The Unforgettable and the Unhoped For

PERSPECTIVES IN CONTINENTAL PHILOSOPHY
John D. Caputo, series editor

1. John D. Caputo, ed., *Deconstruction in a Nutshell: A Conversation with Jacques Derrida.*
2. Michael Strawser, *Both/And: Reading Kierkegaard—From Irony to Edification.*
3. Michael Barber, *Ethical Hermeneutics: Rationality in Enrique Dussel's Philosophy of Liberation.*
4. James H. Olthuis, ed., *Knowing* Other-*wise: Philosophy at the Threshold of Spirituality.*
5. James Swindal, *Reflection Revisited: Jürgen Habermas's Discursive Theory of Truth.*
6. Richard Kearney, *Poetics of Imagining: Modern and Postmodern.* Second edition.
7. Thomas W. Busch, *Circulating Being: From Embodiment to Incorporation—Essays on Late Existentialism.*
8. Edith Wyschogrod, *Emmanuel Lévinas: The Problem of Ethical Metaphysics.* Second edition.
9. Francis J. Ambrosio, ed., *The Question of Christian Philosophy Today.*
10. Jeffrey Bloechl, ed., *The Face of the Other and the Trace of God: Essays on the Philosophy of Emmanuel Levinas.*
11. Ilse N. Bulhof and Laurens ten Kate, eds., *Flight of the Gods: Philosophical Perspectives on Negative Theology.*
12. Trish Glazebrook, *Heidegger's Philosophy of Science.*
13. Kevin Hart, *The Trespass of the Sign.* Second edition.
14. Mark C. Taylor, *Journeys to Selfhood: Hegel and Kierkegaard.* Second edition.
15. Dominique Janicaud, Jean-François Courtine, Jean-Louis Chrétien, Michel Henry, Jean-Luc Marion, and Paul Ricoeur, *Phenomenology and the "Theological Turn": The French Debate.*
16. Karl Jaspers, *The Question of German Guilt.* Introduction by Joseph W. Koterski, S.J.
17. Jean-Luc Marion, *The Idol and Distance: Five Studies.* Translated with an introduction by Thomas A. Carlson.
18. Jeffrey Dudiak, *The Intrigue of Ethics: A Reading of the Idea of Discourse in the Thought of Emmanuel Levinas.*
19. Robyn Horner, *Rethinking God As Gift: Marion, Derrida, and the Limits of Phenomenology.*
20. Mark Dooley, *The Politics of Exodus: Søren Kierkegaard's Ethic of Responsibility.*
21. Merold Westphal, *Overcoming Onto-theology: Toward a Postmodern Christian Faith.*
22. Stanislas Breton, *The Word and the Cross.* Translated with an introduction by Jacquelyn Porter.
23. Edith Wyschogrod, Jean-Joseph Goux, and Eric Boynton, eds., *The Enigma of Gift and Sacrifice.*
24. Jean-Luc Marion, *Prolegomena to Charity.* Translated by Stephen Lewis.
25. Peter H. Spader, *Scheler's Ethical Personalism: Its Logic, Development, and Promise.*

The Unforgettable and the Unhoped For

JEAN-LOUIS CHRÉTIEN

Translated by Jeffrey Bloechl

Fordham University Press
New York
2002

Perspectives in Continental Philosophy No. 26
ISSN 1089–3938

Originally published as *L'inoubliable et l'inespéré* in Paris in 1991
by Desclée de Brouwer.

Library of Congress Cataloging-in-Publication Data

Chrétien, Jean-Louis, 1952–
[Inoubliable et l'inespéré. English]
The unforgettable and the unhoped for / Jean-Louis Chrétien;
translated by Jeffrey Bloechl.
p. cm. — (Perspectives in continental philosophy ; no. 26)
Includes bibliographical references and index.
ISBN 0-8232-2192-X (hardcover)—ISBN 0-8232-2193-8 (pbk.)
1. Memory (Philosophy) 2. Plato I. Title. II. Series.
BD181.7 .C4713 2002
128′.3—dc21 2002000390

Publication of this book was aided by a grant from
The Henry and Ida Wissmann Fund.

Printed in the United States of America
02 03 04 05 06 5 4 3 2 1
First Edition

CONTENTS

TRANSLATOR'S INTRODUCTION

COULD IT BE that the modern forms of thought do not accommodate the full range of human experience? The fact that phenomenology and theology have each answered this question in the affirmative and attempted to correct for the deficiencies of our modernity binds the two fields together at a level deeper and perhaps more important than their many differences. It is true, of course, that theology should exercise caution with the phenomenological "step back" from the faith that nourishes and defines its thinking; it is also true that phenomenology should hesitate before a "theological turn" that promises greater facility describing the experiences of faith but might also bring a diminished facility describing other types of experience. Yet theologians and phenomenologists certainly can agree that the task of thinking is served by an improved means to respect the specificity of religious phenomena. Dissatisfied with a modern rationality that seems unable to speak about such phenomena without occluding them, theologians and phenomenologists have set about the preliminary task of dismantling the inadequate concepts of an entire epoch, with the aim of disabusing us of our predilection for them. In the present work, Jean-Louis Chrétien draws equally on theology and phenomenology, and contributes to their shared effort, with particular concern for the relation between time and being. His point of departure is an analysis of memory, and his immediate concern is to open memory to an immemorial past anterior to any power of the subject. To think that the subject open before any question of closure into itself is to immediately disrupt every claim for self-

The translator wishes to thank Yvette Christofilis for many helpful suggestions and corrections to this English translation.

presence such as contemporary thought has learned to identify as the first and final condition for what it calls the "metaphysics of presence."

The function of memory has been associated with the metaphysics of presence at least since Husserl's lectures on the consciousness of inner time, which depict temporalization as the sheer thrust by which subjective life constitutes itself amid an "original flow," or flux.[1] If this much only defines the present moment as the cusp or leading edge of natural life as it surges forward, additional privileges can be found in a study of memory as re-presentation: to remember, it seems, is to relate to the past from the present moment, which moreover always bathes it in a new light. Together, this means, first, that we are always leaving the immediate milieu behind, and second, that when we turn to look back at it from the present moment, something of it is always lost from view. From this perspective, it may seem that there is something like conception of the "immemorial" past already embedded in Husserl's thinking, but the fact remains that he does not thematize it positively, and in any event the whole of his phenomenology of intentional acts departs from the present moment in which that immemorial is already suppressed. Nothing in the letter of Husserl's text seriously qualifies the view that, for him, the present is the site of the living significance of the past, as indeed it is for the living significance of anything else. Memory, in short, functions under the emprise of a meaning-giving subject that holds every datum in the template of the present.

These elements of Husserl's philosophy have been challenged most forcefully by Emmanuel Levinas, primarily in chapters 2 and 3 of his *Otherwise than Being or Beyond Essence.* There, as elsewhere, Levinas's reading of Husserl is both nuanced and original. He does not doubt, for instance, that Husserl is careful to deny that the "primal apprehension" by which data enter consciousness is in any way an *act,* as if the subject goes out to meet, or worse, seize on an object entering

[1] E. Husserl, *On the Phenomenology of Consciousness of Internal Time (1893–1917),* trans. J. Brough (Boston: Kluwer, 1991). See especially the discussions of "original spontaneity," Appendices 7 and 13.

consciousness.[2] This touches directly on the point, or perhaps moment, in which a datum becomes present in consciousness and in which, simultaneously, the "deep past" (Levinas's expression) slips away. In other words, it touches on the point where Husserl's analyses of time and memory suppress the thought of an immemorial past at the very moment that that thought becomes possible. Opposing himself to Husserl, Levinas argues that that slipping away of the deep past is in fact the occasion and the site of an originary openness at the heart of subjectivity, which for its part is ceaselessly preoccupied with gaining the security of closure. Reinterpreted by Levinas, Husserl's temporal pulsion—and, for that matter, Freudian drive and Spinozist *conatus*—become a blind and misguided flight into being which never pauses, at least under its own power, to welcome the possibility of relief that must be otherwise than being. On Levinas's reasoning, if life is aimed at stability and closure, a relation with the immemorial is thus the source of its constant disturbance. Solitary life is a restless struggle in which every tool or strategy it can employ toward stability is always already disrupted by an anterior bond with what defies them. This seems to define individual existence by an insurmountable predicament: my situation might improve if only I could catch sight of its true nature, yet I myself cannot reach that insight at my own initiative. This conclusion does more than repeat in solemn tones the central assertions of atheist existentialists, since the connection it makes with a fundamental theory of time and subjectivity probably extends the description well into phenomenology and beyond. And, as readers of Levinas know well, the conclusion itself is reinscribed within a notion of promise and hope: all of this restlessness and strife, we are told, is like fitful slumber, until we are awakened by the Other.

The Unforgettable and the Unhoped For attempts this very sort of argument, but draws abundantly on the Platonic and Augustinian currents in which it first appeared. In twentieth-century France, this current has always been strong, even if it

[2] Cf. E. Levinas, *Otherwise than Being or Beyond Essence*, trans. A. Lingis (Boston: Kluwer, 1981), p. 188 n. 14.

has sometimes flowed quietly and along less-frequented byways. Bergson seems to have encountered Neo-Platonism in his reading of Ravaisson, who may have come upon it in his studies of Hegel and Schelling.[3] When Bergson lectured on Plotinus at the Collège de France, his listeners included Emile Bréhier, author of *La philosophie de Plotin* and a major figure in the debate over Christian philosophy which occupied so many French Catholic thinkers during the early 1930s. Platonism and Neo-Platonism are also potent ingredients in the theologies of Daniélou and de Lubac, where Patristic sources are revived to combat a perceived tendency in Scholasticism toward rigid logic and inflexible metaphysics. The prominence of this more deliberate use did not preclude the classical work on texts and their history through which scholars like A. M. J. Festugière, Jean Trouillard, and, to a lesser extent, Pierre Hadot have provided the French intellectual scene with rich, reliable documentation in the area. And for these men, Plotinus was first and foremost a "mystic"[4] and only by extension the source for overcoming onto-theology, such as Pierre Aubenque was to claim in 1969.[5] This way of reading the Neo-Platonists with an eye to contemporary debates defines an important strand in the work of Stanislas Bréton[6] and, along a different route, it virtually sets the agenda for this and other works by Jean-Louis Chrétien.

This is not to say that Chrétien is intent on merely translating the insights of Plotinus, Porphyry, or Proclus, or for that matter Augustine and Philo, into new analyses of select themes, but

[3] H. Bergson, "La vie et l'oeuvre de Ravaisson," in *La Pensée et le mouvant, Œuvres complètes,* vol. 6 (Geneva: Albert Skira, 1946), pp. 237–271.

[4] J. Trouillard, "Raison et negation," in *La Crise de la raison dans la pensée contemporaine* (Paris: Desclée de Brouwer, 1960), p. 34.

[5] P. Aubenque, "Plotin et le dépassement de l'ontologie grecque classique," in *Le Néoplatonisme* Royaumont: Cahiers du colloque Royaumont, 9–13 juin: 101f. The occasion for this effort is at once a wish to evade Heidegger with an emphasis on Plotinian "henology," and the suggestion of an unexpected proximity to Derrida.

[6] For works especially close to Neo-Platonism, see S. Bréton, *Philosophie et mathématique chez Proclus* (Paris: Beauchesne, 1969) and *Matière et dispersion* (Grenoble: J. Millon, 1993). Elsewhere, in his many original works, Bréton's enduring interest in the themes of self-emptying, emptiness, and nothingness exhibit, and often state, an obvious debt to Neo-Platonism.

only to underline the fact that these are the authors to whom he generally turns at the decisive moments in his argument. If he nonetheless avoids an *a priori* commitment to Neo-Platonic or Augustinian thought—and not everyone has thought that he does—this may testify to an overriding concern to simply render a faithful account of certain phenomena such that neither of those two schools, whatever their profundity, can supply entirely on its own. *The Unforgettable and the Unhoped For* is comprised of four dense meditations evoking an experience of time that runs through this world without our catching sight of it, except in rare and exceptional moments. Chrétien is interested in the "extremities" of a past that opens into memory from beyond memory (hence Chrétien's preference for "unforgettable" over "immemorial") and a future beyond either expectation or anticipation ("unhoped for"). This already situates the book close to Levinas in the debate opened with Husserl, but Chrétien does not hesitate to invoke an extraordinary range of classical thinkers in support his argument. Levinas's work contains only hints of the point made here: sometimes what seems new in contemporary philosophy proves on closer inspection to be oldest of all. And from this there follows the possibility that any surprise we might have in learning that, for instance, a theme like the immemorial has been in philosophy since Plato signifies nothing more and nothing less than the unfortunate success of a certain form or phase of thinking which does not know those things. *The Unforgettable and the Unhoped For* calls forth a buried and forgotten strand of our western intellectual tradition, and it often gives the impression that certain forms of thought are simply unsuited to this task of retrieval. This is only one feature of the book that has drawn the enthusiasm of Chrétien's fellow "christian phenomenologists," Jean-Luc Marion and Michel Henry.[7]

[7] Cf. J.-L. Marion, *Étant donné* (Paris: P. U. F., 1997), p. 285; M. Henry, "Speech and Word," in *Phenomenology and the "Theological Turn"* (New York: Fordham University Press, 2000), p. 228. The expression "christian phenomenology" has become common currency in a debate between those who consider it a barbarism and those for whom it signifies the simultaneous fulfillment of both Christian thought and phenomenology.

It is largely due to the impact of Marion's work that this topic of Christianity and phenomenology has gained prominence in recent discussions ranging from the methodological commitments of Husserl and Heidegger to the religious concepts employed by Derrida. As a matter of record, it has been mainly Dominique Janicaud who mentions Chrétien in the company of Marion and Henry (as well as, of course, Levinas), and always with reservations about his claims to describe an originary appeal confirming the inner spirituality of human being.[8] It is not difficult to understand the nature of this objection coming from a scholar of Husserl and Heidegger, even if one does not necessarily agree with it: in order to verify an appeal that would be anterior to any sensibility, intuition, and intention (for only thus could the appeal be *originary*), it will be necessary to suppose the existence and function of a pure receptivity such as phenomenology has resisted since Husserl himself turned to a genetic phenomenology better able to account for the historicity of all experience. In the terms of a more hermeneutic phenomenology, experience is thus context-bound or, if one prefers, inscribed. Needless to say, a book on both the "unforgettable" and the "unhoped for"—indeed, a book intent on establishing their mutual implication—will remind us that this premise of inscribed subjectivity is up for debate not only with regard to our openness/closure to the past, but also our openness/closure to the future. The "eschatological gaze" introduced in the early sections of Levinas's *Totality and Infinity* is never far from Chrétien's analyses of an encounter with the unhoped for, understood as what arrives from beyond expectation and anticipation. And if we accept his argument that this unhoped for is inseparable from the unforgettable, then we must conclude that an argument opposed to the notion of an originary appeal from an unforgettable past is also an argument opposed to an escha-

[8] Cf. D. Janicaud, *The Theological Turn of French Phenomenology*, in *Phenomenology and the "Theological Turn"*, p. 68: "[Chrétien's] thought of the pure promise gives itself off as 'phenomenology' only to reintroduce, subtly but with an altogether strategic constancy, a metaphysics of the secret divine and transcendent call." The reference is to Chrétien's *La voix nue. Phénoménologie de la promesse* (Paris: Eds. de Minuit, 1990).

tological gaze opened by the unhoped for arrival of an immeasurable future. In *The Theological Turn of French Phenomenology,* and even more so in the still-untranslated *La phénoménologie éclatée,* it is clear that Janicaud would be satisfied with a concession that this sort of thinking, while rational enough, is not strictly phenomenological.[9] Yet even this would ask us to look past the most impressive moments in Chrétien's work, where his most poetic and—why not?—religious impulses coincide with his finest phenomenological descriptions in the simplest of examples: exploring the relation of memory and corporeality, chapter 2 pauses over the way one's throat "catches" in the expression of painful recollections, and a note in the "Retrospection" recalls the radiant smile that sometimes transfigures the faces of those whose illness has already ravaged every feature. These are examples of extraordinary richness, delivered with a phenomenological skill that is patent and undeniable. To rule them out of phenomenological inquiry would certainly impoverish the field of its research. This would also lead religious thought back to the difficult suggestion that it may not employ some of the most refined modes of thought without a chaperone. Perhaps it is not yet clear whether this improves on the situation proposed by Heidegger, when he described a theology in need of the clarifications only fundamental ontology could provide[10]—and perhaps it remains an open question, after all this time, whether that proposal actually stands in need of improvement.

The fact that Chrétien is splendidly indifferent to this sort of question is evident wherever he is content to simply follow the force of his argument across divides as allegedly sharp as those that separate Levinas from Heidegger (crossed in chapter 1) or Ancient Greece and medieval Christianity (crossed repeatedly). But again, it is generally to Neo-Platonism that he returns in

[9] D. Janicaud, op. cit., and *La phénoménologie éclatée* (Paris: Eds. de l'éclat, 1998). This is not conceded without some effort. Chapter 5 of the latter book sketches a phenomenology that would be newly reduced ("minimalist") in the wake of lessons drawn from the failed attempt to extend it beyond its proper reach, into theological space.

[10] M. Heidegger, *Phenomenology and Theology,* in *Pathmarks,* ed. W. McNeill (Cambridge: Cambridge University Press, 1998), p. 52.

the end, or more specifically, to strands of Neo-Platonism amenable to the Judeo-Christian worldview with which his "Preface" and "Retrospection" unmistakably identify. At times, the nature of this link can seem to orient the direction of the entire book, as Janicaud has sometimes charged,[11] but without ever coming to the surface. Yet a few exceptions are certainly to be found in brief exercises extracting the forgotten riches of certain ancient terms. Building on the deconstruction of modern conceptions of memory and loss worked out in previous chapters, chapter 3 reinstates a profound sense of "unforgettable" always present but long dormant in the Greek word *alastos* once favored by the tragedians. In chapter 4, it is the Greek *anelpiston,* appearing for instance in Heraclitus's Fragment B18, which yields the precise sense of "unhoped for" necessary for Chrétien's argument. One does not immediately know what to make of this appeal to ancient languages, except perhaps to note that Chrétien's penchant for mining Greek for the linguistic resources needed to express ideas at least sympathetic to the Judeo-Christian tradition certainly belies the simplistic notion that it is the Hebraic world which has been suppressed and forgotten by things Greek and Roman. There is something of this claim in Janicaud's suspicion that certain religious experiences make Chrétien's argument possible, though he stops well short of reducing that argument to a claim for the superiority of Jerusalem over Athens. Basic attention to the text, with its astonishing mixture of references, will have been enough to rule that out. For Chrétien, there is apparently no question of the clean distinction between Jerusalem and Athens one would have to accept before opposing them in such a manner. Reading Chrétien, one thus gains the impression that it is necessary to reconsider Toynbee's influential discussion of distinct experiences of time, with Greek time following an ordered sequence from past to present to future and Hebraic time opened immediately into an immeasurable future.[12] Yet the typology is cer-

[11] Cf., e.g., *supra* note 8.

[12] For this and the following, see A. Toynbee, *An Historian's Approach to Religion* (Oxford: Oxford University Press, 1956), pp. 10–17, 136f.

tainly useful, and to the degree that we are justified in associating Ancient Greece with teleology and the Hebraic world with eschatology, there is some sense in calling the first experience of time "Greek" and second "Hebraic." Moreover, it is also necessary to acknowledge the impact of these theories of time on their respective grammars (or does the influence work in the contrary direction?): whereas the Greek language possesses the tenses necessary to convey an experience of time as discrete units, tense in the Hebrew language conveys action without distinction between past, present, and future. To speak Greek is to pre-apprehend the past or the future from the present moment in which speaks; to speak Hebrew is to bear witness to the eschatological relation with what cannot in any sense be drawn into this present moment.

In the end, when an author like Jean-Louis Chrétien erases these distinctions by finding Greek to say what was reserved for Hebrew, he leads us past the thought that certain languages are incapable of expressing certain things toward the more compelling thought that certain things cannot be contained by any language whatsoever—and that these few things, no less real because they are unspeakable, therefore pressure any and every language from beyond their limits. Speech then—and this is the great assumed thesis of *The Unforgettable and the Unhoped For*[13]—is the very incarnation of spiritual life, at least if the word "spirit" may indicate an attunement to what comes into this life without being contained there. This spiritual dimension of existence, of course, is precisely what is at stake between the "christian phenomenologists" and their critics. If this spiritual dimension of existence is to be rendered intelligible by phenomenological description, must it simply offer itself to intuition and reduction? Perhaps it will be enough for phenomenology to confirm the passage of what remains invisible even while it is sheltered in the visible.

Jeffrey Bloechl
College of the Holy Cross
November 2001

---

[13] *Assumed* only because so many of the earlier works will have worked it out and defended it. See Chrétien's "Retrospection" at the end of this book.

NOTES ON THE TRANSLATION

JEAN-LOUIS CHRÉTIEN'S *L'inoubliable et l'inespéré* presents two special challenges to the translator. The first of these will be evident to any reader of this translation: as Chrétien acknowledges in the retrospective conclusion written for the second French edition (this volume, pp. 119–129), the book is uncommonly rich with references to other authors from a variety of periods and perspectives. While it has been possible to find most, though not all, of these sources in English translation, many of them have a tone and cadence that does not always pass smoothly into the tone and cadence of Chrétien's French, such as it has been reflected in the English. In addition, of course, there are numerous instances where the decisions made in translating a Greek or Latin term into English has not squared with the decisions made in the French translations, which, furthermore, Chrétien frequently adjusts slightly. English translations have thus been cited wherever possible, but rarely without some adjustment to the flow and indeed the content of Chrétien's argument. At risk of monotony, the reader is reminded early and often of the fact that such adjustments have been made.

The second difficulty is precisely what has just been called Chrétien's tone and cadence. As is the case for any translation, certain patterns of expression—in this book, making a point in triplicate, offering a series of formulations that multiply and nuance a single point in one lengthy sentence—that strike one as beautiful in the original may feel awkward or contrived in translation. With regard to Chrétien's work, it is difficult to reduce this problem to matters of style and convention. As this is a point addressed in the translator's introduction to this book, it suffices here to state only that the proximity of spirituality and poetry to what one is perhaps more accustomed to understand as philosophy, has required translation to sometimes stay closer to the movement of the French text than would in other cases seem useful. The requirements of clear English have led to free translation of Chrétien's text on only a few occasions. Similarly, it has only been on rare occasions that that particular French term or set of terms has seemed sufficiently important to inform the reader of their presence in the body of the translation.

PREFACE TO THE SECOND FRENCH EDITION

THIS SECOND EDITION of the present work leaves its body unchanged, but now makes it follow a preface that tempers the abruptness of its opening pages and adds a postface attempting to clarify the general project in which it participates.

This book will undertake a meditation on *loss,* and concentrate on that essential form of the loss that is *forgetting.* A meditation on loss need not be pained or plaintive, but can be joyous and fortifying. Where is the person who need not bid farewell to what, in reality, it is not necessary to lose since, as Rimbaud puts it in his *Illuminations,* it "has departed in affection and new sounds"?[1] But is loss truly loss if we measure and know exactly what we have lost by it, if, while separated from it we nonetheless retain it in memory—if, in other words, the act of losing forms a sovereign act? There is no loss, however much we may have decided for one, without a tearing away *(un arrachement)* that can be neither entirely our own nor entirely transparent to us.

Of all the orders of existence, only a loss can separate us from the origin, from the diverse meanings that the origin can have for us—and from there make it such that we are distinct from it, and thus that we may truly become ourselves. No one can find himself or, before that, seek himself, without having to seek his being lost, which is to say what has been lost. How to exist without fault? And how to proceed without gap, or lack? If this sort of question has numerous metaphysical extensions, one easily grasps in it the opening toward thinking one's birth and early childhood, to a past that is at once our own and remains irreme-

[1] A. Rimbaud, *Illuminations,* in *Œuvres complètes* (Paris: Pléiade, 1954), p. 183.

diably lost, closed to all remembering, such as St. Augustine has been the first to meditate on. The beginning of our history can be recounted only by others, and from the outside: what founds memory is forever closed to memory and forbidden to memory, at least so long as this latter stops short of the raving that comes in the pretense of being more than human. We have begun in loss and forgetting.

But, assuredly, this is not the only form of the *immemorial*, even if it will be the one most easily grasped by everyone. From Merleau-Ponty to Levinas, and indeed other, the question of a past that was never present is of capital importance in contemporary phenomenology, just as it was for Schelling. It is equally important here, and perhaps my title does not indicate sufficiently that the greater part of this book is dedicated to forgetting and its diverse forms. For how to think the unforgettable with any rigor unless one first thinks the forgetting? The book's first chapter shows that this question—exercising a paradoxical allure—of an *originary forgetting* has been posed at the dawn of philosophy, or at its perpetual dawn, with Plato. Attentive study to the Platonic thought of recollection—as well as its interpretations, or misinterpretations, with the passing of time—shows that this first forgetting constitutes its irreducible nucleus. But this forgetting is a forgetting that founds and gives, a forgetting that opens a properly human temporality, which is that of search for the truth and for oneself. Other paths that could have been followed include the theological reflection on a God always already there for us, even when we are not there for God, and the psychological thought of an originary mourning. But to show that a question is originally Platonic is to show that it belongs essentially to philosophy. Moreover, its place in the order of understanding is paramount.

The second chapter gives expression to an astonishment and an interrogation: examination of the philosophical doctrines on forgetting, as diverse and as derivative of contradictory orientations as they may be, show that radical forgetting, forgetting as true loss, involves something intolerable for most thinking. Either it is proposed that there is no definitive forgetting, that by right everything can be recovered, or forgetting is seen as an additive of memory, and it is affirmed that forgetting the non-essential occurs in the service of remembering the essential, assuring its steadiness. This refusal of loss, or of the very possibility of loss is worthy of question. It is of a single piece with the fact that the unforgettable is not a major philosophical concept, for if everything is unforgettable, or if everything that matters is unforgettable, it has nothing specific about it and, in the end, goes without saying. The contrary of this is affirmed in Christianity, with its joyous and affirmative thought of loss, a loss that opens the future. Meditation on the immemorial past and on what is always already lost without return, does not come with any nostalgia: it is rather the basis for a thought of a future which, unlike that of Leibniz, is not inscribed in the present.

With the horizon thus deployed, the two final chapters can set their sights on the two terms giving the book its title and articulation. It is still necessary to specify their range, or span, which is greater than current language accords it. By "unforgettable," we do not mean a punctual event that would escape forgetting by one-knows-not-what privilege of divine right. Experience shows, after all, that people do not cease to forget and to recover what is said to be unforgettable in that particular sense. And by "unhoped for," we do not mean a punctual event by which, without having been expected or thought possible, we will have been pulled from major peril or an inescapable situation. This unhoped for of a single moment is not the unhoped for of always and forever, and to the degree that it withdraws from us in time, and to the degree that the course of our existence is built on it as on a sort of landing, we cease to see it in its own light and sometimes even come to it afterward, to explicate its possibility or probability. These two terms have for us a dimensional character: they aim at that from which such events can be given to us. In this sense, the concept that could unite them is that of the *unceasing:* that which does not cease to come to us, towards us, whether from the past (unforgettable) or from the future (unhoped for).

The present gives a place to the advent of these two movements, as their flow back into our very flesh. And it is only thus that the unforgettable can remain unforgettable and the unhoped for can remain unhoped for. It is only thus that they can, with their sharp light, wound this or that event of our existence, which will remain, if we give our word in its service, its proof and witness: the proof and the witness, and not the unique depository, without which it would only have the evanescent, aesthetic vanity of a "privileged instant" against the background of banality, and thus having its privilege only through banality. Again, it is only in this way that the unforgettable and the unhoped for can belong to our everyday existence and bathe it in their aurora, far from the romantic enchantments whose dissipation only leaves more bitterness.

The *unceasing* has been thought here primarily in the biblical perspective. The Jews are a people of memory only because they are, and only if they are, a people of hope: hope is memory of the promise, conjoining future and past. But philosophy has also known itself to be affected and disturbed by these questions, in so far as it is in its own fashion, since Heraclitus, turned toward the unhoped for.

A preface is only the cradle of a book, letting it glide toward the water and toward the open sea, so that it may begin its crossing. A welcome to those who embark for the second time!

Jean-Louis Chrétien
Paris, November 1999

The Unforgettable and the Unhoped For

1

The Immemorial and Recollection

IS THERE AN INITIAL FORGETTING? Can thought turn toward a radical forgetting that would not presuppose memory and would not consist in interrupting it by adding to or suspending one or another of its powers? When forgetting only indisposes memory—whether this indisposition is enduring or fugitive, slight or serious—it takes all of its meaning from memory, and is essentially subordinate to it, always second and always secondary. It therefore comes too late to found and predetermine. Can one begin from forgetting, with forgetting, and in forgetting? The very possibility of an initial forgetting seems contradictory, which is to say absurd. What could be the meaning of erasing something that has never been inscribed, fixed, or engraved in the first place? What could it mean to obliterate what would not have been marked and remarked, or to cover over what would not be discovered? To begin by forgetting is ultimately to begin from loss, and how could one lose what one did not have to begin with, or what one has not already been? If loss is privation it presupposes, both logically and ontologically, that which is privated. But in this sense, if it is thinkable to begin with the void and emptiness, as the mystics make of the flash of divine Nothingness—pure illumination of the abyss of all beings, and the absolute origin—then it seems absurd to begin from a privation that would, by definition, be belated. What could forgetting deprive us of, if it properly began, and thus would be, still or already, forgetting?

If there is an initial forgetting, what it would make emerge must be an absolute immemorial: not a past that, having been present and thus already open and destined to memory, would afterward become inaccessible in memory or for memory, but a past that is initially past and originally lost: a past that is, in advance and essentially, in withdrawal from all future memory, a past that, simultaneous to its own passage and slipping away, is always already past, always already disappeared, and exists only as having disappeared. Heidegger frequently insisted on the doubling of forgetting: to truly forget, forgetting is not yet enough, for forgetting in memory that one has forgotten is only a mode of remembering—a mode that, precisely, permits us to rediscover what was forgotten. Complete forgetting, he shows, is forgetting the forgetting, disappearance of the very disappearance, where the covering over is itself covered over.[1] This doubling, or second power of forgetting must in truth be posed as first: it is not a higher form of forgetting that succeeds another form exponentially, for the forgetting that does not forget itself constitutes on the contrary a first memory, a first opening to overcoming the forgetting. The same also holds for Socratic ignorance: the ignorance that is ignorant of itself is not an exceptional form of ignorance but is ignorance itself, so that knowledge of our ignorance is the first knowledge and access to all knowing. If there is a first forgetting, it can only be as such: forgetting the forgetting that is itself already and first forgotten, radical immemorial that is radically inaccessible, loss that is lost itself, loss that one cannot even retain as loss, and loss where nothing is lacking and which does not hollow out anything in us that we might wish to fill.

Such a possibility, violently difficult and intensely aporetic, has been thought by Plato in the horizon of what he calls recollection, or *anamnèsis*. This sort of thought is not without tension, and in fact if it represents an essential legacy for Platonists, it would have to be in constituting a perpetual stumbling block for modern interpreters. The study of this thought and of the difficulties that it has stimulated can shed some light on the question of the immemorial. According to it, as put in play by Plato in three of his dialogues—the *Meno*, the *Phaedo*, and the *Phaedrus*—our soul, before incarnation in human form, will

[1] Cf. M. Heidegger, *Vorträge und Aufsätze* (Pfullingen: Neske, 1978), 3:8–9.

have contemplated being and what is true, and it will thus have been charged with an essential knowledge which we will have lost, or rather forgotten, at birth. And learning would thus be nothing other than recollection, just as knowledge in the strict sense would be nothing other than grasping or re-grasping, so that all that is discovered is in fact re-discovered and remembered. This is then related to and mixed with a belief, borrowed from the religious tradition, in the existence of separate souls incarnating or reincarnating, and a thesis on the essence of knowledge, which is to say a philosophical thesis on the proper object of philosophy. At least, this is how these things first appear, which cannot but raise the question of the status of each element, as well as that of their relation. The *Meno* underlines this question by making Socrates's narrative proceed from what he has understood the priests and priestesses to say, to what the divine poets, such as Pindar, affirm in manifesting the identity between knowledge and recollection, to a dialogue on the purely geometrical question of the duplication of the square.[2]

The tension between these two dimensions has not ceased to trouble Plato's readers. It is formulated by Leibniz when he writes, in the preface to his *New Essays on Human Understanding*, that "No one can establish by reason alone how far our past and now perhaps forgotten awareness extended, especially if we adopt the Platonists's doctrine of recollection which, fabulous as it is, is entirely consistent with unadorned reason."[3] For Plato, the question of the limit of forgetting, and thus of the immemorial, would be the place of a coexistence of the mythical and the rational. Can one, must one, seek to separate them, to discriminate one from the other in order to leave this juxtaposition, this hybridization, minimally tolerable to philosophy? For Hegel, too, the Platonic thought of recollection mixes two determinations of memory to be sharply distinguished in meaning and in weight. The notion that to learn is to recollect constitutes, he says, "a maladroit expression, and certainly in this much—that one would reproduce a representation that one has already had

[2] *Meno* 81a–b–c, and 82bf.

[3] G. W. Leibniz, *New Essays on Human Understanding*, trans. and ed. P. Remnant and J. Bennett (Cambridge: Cambridge University Press, 1996), p. 52. [Translation slightly modified. Trans.]

in another time." But memory of the universal can be *Er-innerung*, according to the manner that Hegel understands this word: inwardization, movement toward self, gathering of thought, which is "the profound intellectual sense of the word," and in fact of this thesis.[4] To Leibniz's "fabulous as it is," Hegel responds with the equally conciliatory phrase, "Nevertheless, one cannot deny that in Plato the expression of recollection does not often have the primary, empirical sense."

Recognized by Leibniz and Hegel, this tension belongs to the very topic of Plato's reflections. To suppress it by suppressing one or the other of its terms, as diverse figures in the history of philosophy have not ceased to wish, is perhaps also to deprive this thought of what is its most interrogative feature and most its own. The same Leibniz who points out this tension is also the first to attempt to reduce it,[5] inaugurating the entire modern enterprise of a philosophical re-appropriation of recollection, delivered from its imprisonment in the "fabulous" and returned to its purely rational center. Thus, in the *Discourse on Metaphysics,* he rejoins the thought that says "nothing can be taught to us whose idea we do not already have in our mind," and adds that "this is what Plato so exceedingly well recognized, when he proposed his doctrine of recollection, a very solid doctrine, provided that it is taken rightly, and purged of the error of preexistence . . . ," at which point the *Meno* is explicitly evoked.[6]

[4] "Bei Platon hat jedoch wie nicht zu leugnen ist, der Ausdruck der Erinnerung häutig den empirischen, ersten Sinn," in G. W. F. Hegel, *Vorlesungen über die Geschichte der Philosophie* II, *Werke,* vol. 3 (Frankfurt: Suhrkamp, 1971), p. 45. Cf. *Encyclopedia* § 452. On the word *Er-innerung,* cf. *Phenomenology of Spirit,* trans. A. V. Miller (Oxford: Oxford University Press, 1977), pp. 456 and 492.

[5] Cf. T. Ebert, *Meinung und Wissen in der Philosophie Platons* (Berlin: de Gruyter, 1974), p. 85: "The first to have interpreted recollection as a theory of the pure logical *a priori* is Leibniz." However, Proclus professed respect for such an interpretation. But the paradox is that Leibniz is also the one to have founded, in his philosophy, what in the *Meno* is at the center of myth, namely that what one calls being born, and "what one calls dying" (*Meno* 81b) are not at all the origin and end that one takes them to be. I pre-exist my birth, even if, for Leibniz, this is never in the form of a separated soul. Cf. *Monadology* §§ 72, 73, 76, 77.

[6] Leibniz, *Discourse on Metaphysics and Other Essays,* trans. and ed. D. Garber and R. Ariew (Indianapolis: Hackett, 1991), p. 28.

The "fabulous" could thus be eliminated, by right and with profit. The heart of the thought of recollection becomes the impossibility of learning what this is from the outside, the development of the soul itself from the fore-knowledge that it bears within itself, and which it makes pass from virtual to actual, from confused to distinct. We awaken in time what we know "from all time." With the "fabulous" of recollection, what disappears is nothing other than the temporal comprehension of the *a priori*, and in the same gesture the question of forgetting. My *a priori* knowledge has in no way been received or acquired in an anterior time, but is "from all time"; it belongs to me since I am *(dès que je suis),* without occupying a past. And I do not have to rediscover it, to recapture it, to recollect it to myself, but only to awaken, for it is not forgotten but asleep, or virtual. The purely rational interpretation of recollection forms *the forgetting of forgetting.* With it is effaced the relation between this thought and the immemorial.

What Leibniz affirms in principle, the neo-Kantians would show the whole length of their penetrating and meticulous interpretations of the works of Plato. Hence does Nicolai Hartmann, in his *Platos Logik des Seins,* write: "With this theory where learning occurs by recollection, the thought becomes quite clear that there must be a knowledge that has an origin other than that which is found in the individual existence of things. And it is on this knowledge that true understanding must be founded." This makes it a science quite distinct from opinion. "For it has its foundation assured in what consciousness draws from itself, in what Plato calls, in mythical fashion, 'recollection', but which we certainly can, in a more modern terminology, characterize as *a priori*. The very appeal that Plato makes to mathematics justifies this interpretation of recollection."[7] Such a reduction of recollection to the *a priori* is also

[7] Hartmann's *Platos Logik des Seins* appeared in 1909, in a collection edited by H. Cohen and P. Natorp. It has been republished in 1965 (Berlin: de Gruyter). See pp. 180–181. To our knowledge, it is also the first to translate the Greek *alèthéia,* truth, as *Unverborgenheit* (unconcealment), as Heidegger would later do.

one of the guiding threads of Paul Natorp's majestic *Platos Ideenlehre.*[8]

What is there that is truly great in Plato? "He has been called," writes Natorp, "the divine Plato; but precisely what one finds in him that is so divine may in fact be the most human of his weaknesses." This is what renders Plato mythical and mystical. What constitutes his grandeur does not lie there, but rather in "the discovery of the *a priori.*" And it is with regard to the *Meno,* where the discovery would be made, that Natorp affirms, "The grandeur, if anywhere there is one, lies here in simplicity; the simple is the great in so far as it is the radical." In what does it consist? "The famous phrase in the *Meno* on knowledge as 'recollection' signifies in reality: conduction of understanding back . . . to its source in consciousness of self." This latter has the law-like form that constitutes the pure content of consciousness. "This is the ultimate meaning of the Platonic 'Idea'."[9] And the "complete mythical and mystical covering of the doctrine of recollection" must be abandoned, for in the end, this is only "poetic ornament."[10] Such, at least, is the view of Natorp, himself too good a reader of Plato and too good a philosopher not to recognize that there is in Plato's own work, and just where he, Natorp, finds "the historical origin of the *a priori,*" a certain "psychological and finally metaphysical" torsion.[11] This "psychological apriorism" is rejected by Aristotle "without suspecting its more profound tendency"[12]: it is only the most external appearance of the discovery of the true *a priori.* For all that, Natorp sees no real need for such a correction of Plato, nor for a purification of the theory of recollection of its mythical aspects, for this movement of rectification would be at work already in the dialogues themselves. According to Natorp, in the maieutics

[8] P. Natorp, *Platos Ideenlehre* (Hamburg: Meiner, 1994; first edition, 1902). The (significant) *subtitle* is *Eine Einführung in den Idealismus,* an introduction to idealism.

[9] Ibid., respectively, pp. 37, 42, 34, and 29.

[10] Ibid., p. 36; cf. p. 70.

[11] Ibid., pp. 143, 145.

[12] Ibid., p. 396. On the positively stupefying height from which Natorp treats Aristotle, as Brunschvicg would later do in France, see p. 147.

of the *Theatetus*—in the art of spiritual midwifery of which Socrates forcefully avails himself—in helping the other to deliver and to bring to light the thoughts that are already his or her own, "we immediately see a new and very pure transformation of the theme of recollection."[13] The "consciousness"[14] in dialogue with itself that we are to see in the *Theatetus* would be "the clear and pure expression, this time kept pure of everything mythical and mystical, of *a priori* understanding." The *Symposium* would also succeed with such a purification of the thought of the pure, that is to say of the *a priori.* In effect, what Natorp considers insufficient and unsatisfying in the doctrine of recollection is that "pure fundamental concepts" are finally found "given in 'preliminary fashion,' and are not produced in pure fashion from the beginning."[15] The *a priori* itself thus would possess a facticity that is insupportable within transcendental idealism, since that which I recollect, the Ideas, has been seen again, seen simply, and received in contemplation, and since "consciousness" would only rediscover them as a fact. The *Symposium* would have overcome this facticity.

Indeed, in the fact that "what Eros ultimately wishes is not the beautiful" but "generation in beauty," Natorp sees the accomplishment of "an overcoming of the psychological meaning of the Idea as *a priori* understanding." The *Symposium* would come finally to show that understanding of the Ideas is not at all due to "seeking in a beyond, whether this is before birth or after death, no more than it is only the rediscovery of a representation that one had already possessed in some preliminary fashion, such that it lay available but *simply* asleep": this understanding would be in contrast with the understanding produced in the spontaneous activity of consciousness that lives only in

[13] Ibid., p. 101.

[14] The identification of *psukhè,* of the Platonic soul, with the consciousness and self-consciousness of modern metaphysics is the constant and untenable presupposition of Natorp's work. In this regard, see M. Heidegger, *Prolegomena to the History of the Concept of Time,* trans. T. Kisiel (Bloomington: Indiana University Press, 1985), p. 73.

[15] Natorp, *Platos Ideenlehre,* p. 145.

renewing itself by itself. Thus would come to light "not the suppression, but the ultimate deepening and the ultimate purification of the theme of recollection," in the form of a thought of the productivity of consciousness. It does not discover and does not rediscover; it produces. "Is it not necessary to say that here the 'metaphysical' *a priori* is overcome by the transcendental *a priori*?"[16]

When recollection is understood in this way, there can no longer be any question of a past, a forgetting, or an immemorial. The identification of the Platonic Idea with the *a priori* of transcendental idealism leads to the paradoxical consequence that it suppresses all reference to anteriority, to what is already—always already—there. Yet this anteriority is evoked by the very expression *a priori*, and reading Plato in light of Kant will be meaningless unless Plato is permitted to interrogate, in turn, Kant himself, and in the context of thinking about the temporal sense of the *a priori*. Theodor Ebert rightly said that: "In reality, if the meaning of reminiscence must be a theory of the *a priori*, then the metaphor of recollection, with its temporal implications, is a circumstantial masquerade, if not misleading."[17] Now, in the Platonic thought of recollection, it is properly the "fabulous" that expressly poses the temporal dimension of knowledge, understood as knowledge of the non-temporal. To reduce the inner tension of this thought amounts to losing what is most precious to it, and to submitting it to the common denominator of modern idealism.

The paradox inherent to the interlacing of the "fabulous" and the rational is brought out by Leibniz. It is that of the *first time* of knowledge, of first knowing. To learn is nothing other than to recollect, but if there has been a first knowing, then that which is recollected and remembered, cannot itself have first been recollected. This first knowing thus contradicts the same thesis on the essence of knowledge that it serves to found. Plato himself seems to lend support to this paradox in the page from the *Phaedo* where he evokes, in order to exclude it, what will

[16] Ibid., pp. 178–179.
[17] Ebert, *Meinung und Wissen in der Philosophie Platons*, p. 86.

thenceforth be called "innatism": he employs the term 'learning' to designate the acquisition of first knowledge, that which precedes our birth and which our birth makes us forget. "Will one thus recollect what one has learned *(emathon)* at a given moment?—Necessarily."[18] Of this phrase, Jacob Klein writes in his commentary on the *Meno*: "In spite of the recollection thesis, the soul itself is thus understood to be capable of, and at some period of time actually to have been engaged in, *learning*"[19]—without this learning having been a recollection. In his *New Essays on Human Understanding*, Leibniz would show forcefully that the thesis of the pre-existence of souls only postpones the problem of knowledge, and that unless one is willing to enter an infinite regress, only innatism, which escapes the aporia of the first time, is coherent. "It is easy to judge," he writes, "that the soul must have already had innate knowledge in its preceding state (if preexistence took place), however remote it may be, just as it does here." The fact that one always supposes an anterior state does not change the fact that "it is obvious that some self-evident truths must have been present in all these states."[20] The myth of the pre-existence of souls would thus succeed to an ineluctable contradiction, escaping the thought of knowledge that it pretends to support. And by every appearance, there is nothing rational in that thought that is better founded by innatism or by a thought of the *a priori*, which would avoid, above all, fabulous constructions, but also, ultimately, superfluous and contradictory ones. To what end would one thematize the *already* in the fact that I always already know, and assign a time to the *in advance* evident in the fact that I know in advance, or *a priori*? Does it not belong to the very economy of rational thought to content itself with what I always know, even if virtually or obscurely? Why should myth give figure to the unrepresentable immemorial?

---

[18] *Phaedo* 76c, on "innatism"; cf. 76a.

[19] J. Klein, *A Commentary on Plato's Meno* (Chicago: The University of Chicago Press, 1989; first edition, 1969), p. 131. Cf. p. 166: "Whenever learning is identified with recollection . . . the problem of *initial* learning is held in suspense." The whole question is to think this "suspense" philosophically.

[20] Leibniz, *New Essays on Human Understanding*, trans. Remnant and Bennett, p. 30.

The same definitions of Plato where the neo-Kantians saw confirmation of their interpretation underline what is in fact an essential difference: "The act of recovering the science in oneself is precisely recollection, is it not?" says the *Meno.* And the *Phaedo* tells us: "What we call learning will be the recovery of our own science."[21] It is certainly correct to insist on the propriety of this science and on the self that recollects it, in so far as the doctrine of recollection is opposed to any introduction of exterior knowledge into the soul, but leaves entirely in the dark the meaning of this propriety and of the being of this self. The *re-* of the recovery, the *ana-* of *analambanein,* is the very heart of the thought of recollection in its temporal interpretation. That the *self* is recovered by science also signifies that the self is what *recovers* knowledge. If "the truth of beings is always in our soul,"[22] the comprehension of this *always* and of being *in the soul* is also what decides this truth, and any possible identification with the *a priori* of idealism. The weight of the *recovery* is precisely what the mythical representations put in evidence. The forgetting of forgetting in the modern interpretations is of a single piece with a failure to understand here that the self is not self-evident. It is not a matter of a thesis on knowledge that would presuppose the perfect clarity of what it is to be a self, but an interrogation that puts in question and in play what it is, and thus also what it costs, to be a self. Far from being an arbitrary explication by way of gratuitous constructs, myth is here what shatters the false evidences prevailing over the self.

For science proper, *oikeia epistèmè,* what we recapture in recollection would not be something added to the self and the possession of which or loss of which leaves the self unaltered and intact in its being. If this science is what first and above all is, in this life, by reason of forgetting, inaccessible to us, this forgetting also forms a forgetting of self. The forgetting of self

[21] *Meno* 85d and *Phaedo* 75e. [Here and elsewhere, it has been necessary to adjust the English text of Plato's *Collected Works* consulted for this translation (eds. Hamilton and Cairns, Princeton: Princeton University Press, 1963) in conformity with the French translation provided by Chrétien. Trans.]

[22] *Meno* 86b.

necessarily alters the self in some way. It could not be a simple metaphorical expression of the virtuality of an *a priori* not yet rendered conscious. For this forgetting expels not only a past, but an *other past,* a past other than any past where I am already human, a past other than any past of this incarnate life. Now this other past—absolute, non-empirical, always already forgotten—is nonetheless that which opens me to the truth of being, and thus what alone can make of me what I am and what I am in so far as human. Being human must be problematic in relation to the self, for I can think who I am, as place of knowledge, open to the truth, only with reference to the time when I was not—not yet human. Plato points this out frequently. The *Phaedo* evokes the soul, ours or that in which we have a share, "before it was born in this human form."[23] The expression is taken up elsewhere in various modes. The *Meno* also evokes the time in which one of the interlocutors "was not human."[24] The other past would be that time. The institution of our humanity thus lies together with the institution of forgetting. What makes us humans what we are is having always already forgotten being, and in such a way that this forgetting neither abolishes nor effaces our relation to being, but forms on the contrary an inalienable modality of being. According to the *Meno,* the totality of time is shared between a time when we are human and a time when we are not. Always knowing, having always known: this is knowing sometimes humanly and sometimes inhumanly. But this knowledge that precedes being human *in us* is also what founds our humanity. The myth in the *Phaedrus* affirms: "every human soul has, by reason of her nature, seen true being; else would she never have entered into this human being."[25] In the sense that Littré's French dictionary gives to the word "immemorial," it is "what is so ancient, that it leaves no memory." The immemorial is what we lived before being human, and in order to finally be human, to be able to be human: what in us overcomes the human and exceeds it is what alone renders us

[23] *Phaedo* 72e, 73a; cf. 76c.
[24] *Meno* 26a.
[25] *Phaedrus* 249e.

human. There is an immemorial only for us humans and by us. This dimension radically separates the thought of recollection from that of the *a priori*.

Now, if recollection aims to make us recapture what we have always known and always, as humans, forgotten, if it draws back the forgetting of being, it in no way consists in making us rescind time, and it does not have as its end making us become once again what we were before, when we knew for the first time. Were we to do that, we would cease to be human. For Plato, recollection is the properly human modality of knowledge, and not the reestablishment of a state anterior to humanity. Equally at stake in the *Meno* is a relation to the future. Plato says not only that finding the truth is recollection, but also that "seeking and learning are in fact nothing but recollection."[26] The immemorial of a knowledge that one must recapture by uprooting forgetting is what gives us the future; it is what opens a future where rediscovering is not repeating, and where the second time of recollection does not at all reproduce the first, antenatal time. The absolute and pre-human past of the first vision produces the human future, granting it its perpetual resource. In this sense, we re re-collect ourselves only to the future, in seeking. A purely pragmatic interpretation of myth[27]—making its sole meaning reside in what, both in fact and in act, invites us to seek—forgets the forgetting, and it forgets the eschatological character of recollection, thought from the extremities of time. These extremities are not symmetrical: we can and must always seek and always learn what is not yet known, in human time and according to the human future, indefinite and finite at once, by reason of the fact that all seeking is built on to a past that is absolute and other than human. We are the future of the absolute past, the future of the immemorial, and it is in this that it gives us what is ours concerning thought. All these determinations of Platonic recollection show that in it there is indeed a self, and that that self is properly in question.

---

[26] *Meno* 81d.

[27] This is the weakness of Jacob Klein's otherwise remarkable interpretation. Cf. *A Commentary on Plato's Meno*, pp. 168f.

The thought of knowledge as recollection does not lead to an exercise of memory, but to an exercise of anticipation. It is not in any way a matter of becoming able to remember what it is that took place in the past, nor of what we ourselves were in an anterior state.[28] Memory forms rather more of an obstacle to recollection than an aid to it—and this we can see in the way the *Meno* opposes the young slave, who in this life has not studied, has learned nothing, and has therefore neither retained nor revivified anything in and by his memory, thus the man of empty memory, to Meno himself, enamored of doctrines and citations, always eager to extend his memory of formulas and new theses. The former will be the only one in this dialogue to recollect and thus learn some truth, whereas the second, in spite of all Socrates's efforts, will show himself to be inept, and will leave, in a sense, just as he came.[29] Socrates himself, man of recollection, frequently presents himself to be without memory or its power of retention.[30] The way of recollection, just like the way of love, begins with emptiness and dispossession, and not with the accumulation of rediscovered or re-conquered memories. In Socrates's exchange with Meno's young slave, where it is a matter of doubling the surface of a given square, and of finding the line that permits this, the latter proposes two responses whose falsity Socrates makes him discover. When Socrates repeats the initial question, the boy affirms: "As for me, I do not know." At these words, Socrates turns to Meno and tells him: "Observe, Meno, the stage he has already reached on the way of recollection."[31] The fact that he has progressed in recollection is attested only in his avowal of ignorance: at that moment, he has not yet recollected anything. He has no more resolved the problem posed to him than he had before, and he thus remains at the point of departure, yet he is said to have advanced. How

[28] Cf. J.-P. Vernant, *Mythe et pensée chez les Grecs,* vol. 1 (Paris: Maspero, 1965), pp. 103–105.

[29] All of this has been well analyzed by Jacob Klein, op. cit., and by Rémi Brague, *Le restant* (Paris: Vrin, 1978).

[30] *Meno* 71c–d; *Hippias Minor* 368d; *Protagoras* 334c–d and 336d.

[31] *Meno* 84a. Translations differ in using "way" or "route" [or, in English, "path". Trans.] for the Greek *badizôn*.

could one advance in recollection without recollecting? As soon as he knows that he does not know, as soon as he is disabused of his first errors, he will seek willingly, and is therefore in the disposition required to truly seek.[32] It is the desire for knowledge and the tension of the search for it that constitute progress in recollection. And this shows clearly that its proper temporal dimension is the future—the opening and the gift of the future.

What must always come for us, must and can be regained by us. In desiring to know it, we are already there, by anticipation. No lost time has ever, nor ever will be regained: time is given—that of the truth of what we are and are not. The other past, the absolute past, will remain forever an absolute past; it will not be recaptured or rediscovered, or re-presented, rendered present again. It does not come back as what may be repeated or reproduced. However, it does come back to us from the future *(depuis l'avenir):* what in the past made us comes back to us, it befalls to us, in and as the task of being. We go toward the immemorial without returning to it by somehow turning ourselves toward the past. In other words, recollection does not turn back across forgetting. To traverse forgetting is not to abolish it. We do not recollect ourselves, but only our being. The veil of forgetting that covers it is lifted by recollection, lifted little by little, step by step, temporally, and not by sudden illumination. The intelligible forms are not regained by us according to their precession. They are always already there; the moment we see them they have always already been there. But nothing of *our* past is remembered: we see what is made forgotten, but we do not get back before the forgetting, and nothing of our own forgetting—the acts and experiences by which we forgot—is as such abolished. In an empirical forgetting, I can, by reminding myself of what I had forgotten, also come to remember having forgotten, the time when I forgot, and the causes or circumstances that led me to forget. Not only can I lift the veil, I can in some way remember the veiling itself. A forgetting can itself be dated, even if it always remains as such non-representable. But concerning an initial forgetting, a for-

[32] *Meno* 84b–c.

getting that founds our life, a forgetting that is in solidarity with incarnation and birth, nothing of this order can occur: I could never remind myself of my anterior lives, nor of having contemplated ideas before taking body, nor of being born and, indeed, of being born having forgotten. The forgetting according to which I have always already forgotten, the forgetting before all memory, forgetting without date, forgetting by which there is the immemorial, always remains immemorial. Far from abolishing it, Platonic recollection shows, on the contrary, its irreducible force. Kierkegaard ironizes about the pretended memory of anterior lives, writing: "He related to me what he had been before becoming himself."[33] I before I *(moi avant moi),* what I did before beginning and in beginning will not be regained, and need not be. The initial forgetting and the initial loss will not be repaired, and their primacy is of such a nature that I could never take it back into myself, nor coincide with it, rendering it in thought and thus becoming its contemporary. No rebirth repeats birth. My own immemorial remains forever forgotten and lost.

Remembering does not conduct one to plenitude: it is not some kind of recapitulation, some complete gathering of my history, in full and definitive grasp such that my end would rejoin my founding principle. The Platonic myths do not depart from a primordial facticity: far from delivering themselves from it, they state it, as they alone can do. To state mythically the first time of knowledge, the first knowledge, is equivalent to making it renounce philosophy and showing why it must do so. Its beginning is charged with the ballast of an immemorial past; it does not begin by the absolute past that it represents as always already lost, escaping every repetition and every representation; it begins with a second time, which alone counts for it, thus it begins in pulling itself together. Proclus has underlined forcefully that "What we recollect is not accompanied by the memory of the time in which we have learned it, so that recollection

[33] S. Kierkegaard, *Philosophical Fragments,* in *Kierkegaard's Writings*, vol. 7, trans. H. Hong and E. Hong (Princeton: Princeton University Press, 1985), p. 91. This work constitutes *a contrario* one of the strongest modern meditations on Platonic reminiscence.

itself obviously has a specific time."[34] Just as the immemorial—as my absolute past, my past which cannot be rendered present and which for me, for the one who writes or speaks here, never could be present—does not include the time of my historical life, so the immemorial has for me something excessive about it, an excess that founds me, that sends me and destines me, and is known to me only obliquely, in the excess of being. It is not directly thematized.

At the end of the argument for recollection, the *Phaedo* shows this clearly. At that point, the necessity of the existence of the soul before our birth is proposed as equal to the necessity of the Ideas, or of the being *(ousia)* which is in question there.[35] But only the necessity of the Ideas permits thinking the necessity of this pre-existence, by reason of the kinship between the soul and the forms. The always already present Ideas are the *ratio cognoscendi* of the always already of the soul, and not the inverse. The abyss of our past opens on another abyss that alone permits us to know it. We cannot recollect ourselves such as we always already were, but we do not cease to recollect ourselves from being. The immemorial of the truth is one with the profundity of the future: being is always already turned toward us, open for us, and every initiative that we can take is preceded and outstripped by it; there is always a lag *(retard)* in the initiative, a lag that is constitutive and does not lend itself to any measure. But this delay that nothing will abolish does let its face appear in expectation: the truth of being awaits us and calls to us from far in our future. In this respect, the erotic recollection depicted in the *Phaedrus* does not present a meaning otherwise than is presented in the mathematical anamnesis of the *Meno*: it does not make one rediscover souls that would have been

---

[34] Proclus, *Sur le Premier Alcibiade de Platon,* vol. 2, ed. and trans. A. Segonds (Paris: Les Belles lettres, 1986), p. 251. [English translations of Proclus on Plato are rare and difficult to come by. It has therefore seemed best to translate the French texts that Chrétien has employed, and, moreover, sometimes modified. In this case, the English translation by W. O'Neill, *Alcibades I* (The Hague: Nijhoff, 1965) has been consulted here and below (notes 80, 84), but found to differ significantly from the sense of Chrétien's French text. Trans.]

[35] *Phaedo* 76d–77a.

already encountered once, in the mysterious time, long ago, of another life—as in romantic conceptions of fated love—but makes souls find themselves in meeting themselves for the first time, in rediscovering and recollecting the beautiful. It weights the irreducible newness of the encounter with immemorial beauty. Every encounter rediscovers. It does not rediscover what it encounters, which is always original *(inédit),* but rediscovers in encountering and encounters in rediscovering, without confusing the two any more than one might confuse light with what it illumines. In the *Phaedrus,* the amorous encounter, as the site of recollection, does not for all that lead to reproduction or repetition, but on the contrary to the future opened by love, the future of truth and experience, of the olympian struggle[36] taken up in the only truly olympian games—those of life itself. The *Phaedrus* is the only one of Plato's dialogues where the future of the amorous encounter is presented as eschatological. Those who are in love in this life are dedicated to remain united and in solidarity even after death—something that the *Symposium*, for example, does not affirm. Affirmation of the unforgettable character of love for someone, beyond even death, is one with the thought of love as recollection, with the immemorial delivery *(envoi)* of the beautiful. The *forever* of love translates, at the other extremity of time, into the *always already* of the immemorial.

Without meditating directly on the temporal significance of Platonic recollection, Kant has interpreted it wholly otherwise than the neo-Kantians. For Kant, it was not a matter of a mythical clothing of the *a priori* such as he understood it. For him, recollection is an example of the *Schwärmerei,* of religious exaltation.[37] Yet this *Schwärmerei,* he also says, bears paradoxical witness to the philosophical and mathematical superiority of Plato. Excelling in both of these two orders, Plato is seized, when coming before the power attested by the deployment and extension of mathematical knowledge, by an "admiration" be-

---

[36] *Phaedrus* 256b.

[37] I. Kant, *Vom einem neuerdings erhobenen vornehmen Ton in der Philosophie,* in *Werke,* vol. 3 (Darmstadt: Insel, 1958), p. 380 (*Akademie Textausgabe,* vol. 8, p. 392).

yond what could ever be experienced by the "simple mathematician," who is absorbed in the object to the point of failing to ask about the power of the knowing subject, or the "simple philosopher," who sees metaphysics only as a superior physics. Only this admiration "drives him," writes Kant, "to the conception that takes all of this knowledge not for acquisitions made recently in our earthly life, but for the simple revival of ideas that are indeed anterior, and whose foundation could be nothing less than kinship with divine understanding."[38] Only *a priori* intuitions, and not concepts, permit the extension of pure reason *(connaissance),* and they alone can make it progress, as takes place in mathematics, without recourse to experience. Plato's error will have been a failure to discern the sensible nature of the *a priori* intuitions—space and time—of having attributed them to understanding, and having thus attempted to account for this power by appeal to recollection, seeking "pure intuition in divine understanding and its archetypes."[39] Plato's "admiration" would thus be one with the "finality" that seems intent on certain representations especially well suited for resolving a multitude of problems.

The *Critique of Judgment* deepens this thought. What is it in geometry that has excited Plato's admiration *(Bewunderung),* which through a "misunderstanding" originating from the fact that the "critical use of reason" has not yet been established,[40] opens him to *Schwärmerei*[41]? An overabundance, an excess of meaning in the properties of representations; the encounter, in what is necessary, with an unexpected meaning and fecundity that seem rather to have expected us, to have been in expecta-

[38] I. Kant, *Welches sind die werklichen Fortschritte, die die Metaphysik seit Leibnitzens und Wolffs Zeiten in Deutschland gemacht hat?*, in *Werke*, vol. 3, p. 665.

[39] Kant, *Vom einem neuerdings erhobenen vornehmen Ton,* in *Werke,* vol. 3, p. 379 (*Akademie Textausgabe,* vol. 8, pp. 391–392).

[40] I. Kant, *Kritik der Urteilskraft,* § 62, *Akademie Textausgabe,* vol. 5, p. 365. For an English translation of this section of Kant's third *Kritik,* see *Critique of Judgment,* trans. J. H. Bernard (New York: MacMillan, 1951), pp. 208–212. [It has sometimes been necessary to modify this translation significantly. The Akademie Textausgabe pagination, which is noted in the body of this translation, is therefore cited in the following six notes. Trans.]

[41] Ibid., p. 364.

tion of our thought—"the very necessity of what is purposive and is constituted as if it were intended by design for our use,"[42] the *a priori* purposiveness of representations "for all sorts of cognitive uses, this purposiveness being quite unexpected due to the simplicity of their construction,"[43] "that which one did not think."[44] The unexpected, the unforeseen, the unhoped for character of an overabundance of meaning is the proper object of admiration. This is why Kant expressly distinguishes it from astonishment *(Verwunderung).* Astonishment excites a doubt that things really are as such, a doubt whether I have seen well or judged well. In contrast, admiration is "astonishment that always returns *(eine immer widerkommende Verwunderung)* despite the dissipation of this doubt."[45] Such is this overabundance, which for us always remains overabundance, that Plato has been able to explain it only by our "intellectual affinity with the origin of all beings."[46] For Kant, the fact that the unhoped for reflects the immemorial constitutes the mark of its grandeur, even if this same grandeur gets lost. The perpetual return of admiration before the opening, as if already welcoming, of the future of reason takes note of an immemorial past. Taking note of it is not returning to it.

The time in which I was not yet human, the time before my birth, lost for me through my birth, will remain irremediably lost, and will never be regained as such. Yet everything that I recognize and recapture for the first time, but a first time that is also a second time, is rendered possible only by this loss. I am always already in the truth, which is itself always and forever. But for human beings, this "always already" is that of forgetting: the immemorial consecrates it to the future, it comes from the future itself, though without ceasing to be immemorial and without us being able to either return to the origin of our being or coincide with it. For Plato, the vocation of knowledge, the call of truth and to truth, can be thought only as the excess of a

[42] Ibid., p. 363.
[43] Ibid., p. 366.
[44] Ibid., p. 363.
[45] Ibid., p. 365.
[46] Ibid., p. 363.

past that is radically lost. As my own past, this lost past gives myself to myself in so far as I recognize and recapture the truth. I am always a step behind the advent of the truth, and I am its contemporary only in coming to it. As Heidegger has said, *anamnèsis* names well the relation of being to the being, and does not designate a recollection that would be psychological.[47] But according to this relation, to be a self amounts to not being able to coincide with one's own origin, being unable to appropriate what is properly our own. This is what stands in the way of tracing the thought of recollection back to a naïve and awkward formulation of innatism or transcendental idealism. What it has of the mythical does not represent some contingent clothing of a pure rational content, any more than it does a simple exhortation that exhausts its meaning in the very effort of knowing. It thinks what other thoughts live to forget: the temporal extremities that found human knowledge, and the charge of the immemorial by which we are opened to the truth in a fashion such as we ourselves could never have begun to open. And for all of that, this absence of beginning is neither non-temporality nor eternity.

What then, having said all this, is myth? For Plotinus, the myth, far from corresponding—as hasty theories would have it—to a power of unification, assembly, and totality, is on the contrary analytic: it distinguishes, separates, divides, and distributes in time and according to the time that is eternally united in it. The task of interpretation is therefore not to analyze, but on the contrary to assemble and reunite what a myth analyzes and divides, in composing *sunairesis,* or "syneresis."[48] Is such

---

[47] M. Heidegger, *Parmenides,* trans. A. Schuwer and R. Rojcewicz (Bloomington: Indiana University Press, 1992), p. 124. Heidegger objects to translating this term as *Er-innerung* or *Wiedererinnerung,* both of which risk favoring a psychological interpretation.

[48] Cf. Plotinus, *Enneads* III, 5, 9, trans. S. MacKenna (New York: Penguin, 1991), pp. 185–186. [The term "syneresis" is employed by linguists and chemists to designate a process of contraction. Trans.] [It has sometimes been necessary to modify MacKenna's translation significantly, chiefly where its tendency to suggest that Plotinian thought appeals to the experiences of the elect places it at odds with the somewhat different notion put forth in Chrétien's analysis. Trans.]

an assembly possible for the myth of recollection? Or is its meaning, properly speaking, impossible to extract in such a manner? Its object is nothing other than the temporality of knowledge in so far as it cannot be fully gathered into place, which is to say in so far as it cannot be reduced to the coincidence and transparency of a pure presence. To submit it to such a procedure would thus be to destroy it, to lose its very meaning, to lose what in it cannot be said temporally. It states the past of knowledge, of knowing, the other past of knowledge as what the future gives, through forgetting. This past does not bear a parousia. Whatever the origin and nature of the religious traditions of which Plato makes use in this myth, he has without any doubt detoured and re-routed them toward philosophy, for the very object of recollection is not of the order of religion, but is the truth of being toward which science and philosophy struggle. Our relation to non-temporal truth is itself irreducibly and insurpassably temporal. The time in which we were not yet human founds, as a matter of knowledge, the possibility of human time, but it cannot be regained or repeated in human time. Human time begins by forgetting this other time, but this forgetting cannot be reduced to mere privation or to a lack of memory: it is what renders possible any memory of the truth as regaining the truth. Emmanuel Levinas has recognized that "the immemorial past is intolerable for thought,"[49] thus revealing the novelty of his own project. This requires us to ask whether Plato founds the very possibility of thought on the immemorial past.

For Plato, forgetting is fundamental in human time itself. The *Symposium* founds the care and study of knowledge on its constant flight and perpetual exodus in forgetting: *lèthè gar épistèmès exodos.*[50] Our knowledge of the same can remain the same only through acts that are always new, through a constant renewal of our acts of understanding. To retain a memory through time is to always exercise new acts of remembering.

[49] E. Levinas, *Otherwise than Being or Beyond Essence,* trans. A. Lingis (Boston: Kluwer, 1978), p. 199 n. 21.

[50] *Symposium* 208a.

For mortals, there is an essential identity between maintaining and renewing. Fidelity requires one to reassert the act at each new instant. We do not cease to rejuvenate[51]—not to become younger than we were, but to remain the same. Now, if the content of the knowledge that slips away remains the same, the act by which I first understand it is irremediably in flight, lost. The renewal does not deny and does not abolish the exodus, but on the contrary takes note of its necessity. The mortal exists and continues to exist only in the mode of saving and safeguarding itself, in always giving itself again and anew what it does not cease to lose. There is nothing accidental about this forgetting; it founds the proper modality of our relation to the truth. Only a being that is essentially forgetful of truth can have to remember it. In the situation evoked by the *Symposium,* I can remember my acts anterior to my understanding, in so far as they are mine, even if they cannot return—which could not be done in relation to pre-existence. But whether one does or does not intervene in pre-human time, it remains the case that the exposure to forgetting, in so far as it places our being principally in peril, is nevertheless the primary form of our exposure to being and truth. For us, all truth is exposed to the peril of forgetting, and we relate to it only in and through this same peril. A human being is not only being in peril, perilous being, but also the very peril of being, that in which being risks itself. "Forgetting" is an essential name of this peril.

Everything begins with this forgetting in so far as it is the loss of the origin. But the traversal of forgetting in recollection, not forgetting the forgetting itself, does not take us back to the origin and it does not permit us to regain it, as if the forgetting, after having been crossed, had never truly taken place. Recapturing the truth forms a modality specific to our relation to it: this is not to grasp it once again as in the first time, but in a wholly different manner. The force of the thought of recollec-

---

[51] *Symposium* 207d, *Neos aei gignomenos.* This formula is heavy with the sense in which Aristotle uses it to characterize the temporality proper to . . . plants. Cf. *Parva naturalia* 467a 12f. On the aspect of renewal in memory, cf. Proclus, *Commentaire sur la République,* vol. 3, trans. A. Festugière (Paris: Les Belles lettres, 1970), p. 307.

tion is also to be measured by what it renounces: it renounces making the first time of knowledge, our first access to the truth, an object for philosophy as such. For its part, philosophy presupposes that first access as its other past, the absolute past that myth alone can express. The original opening to the truth cannot be thought according to the presence of the present. This once again marks an irreducible difference with transcendental idealism and its "original acquisition,"[52] where spirit gives itself to itself what innatism thinks as given. There is indeed an "original acquisition" for Plato, but this origin is always already forgotten and lost.

When Plotinus takes up the Platonic thought of recollection, he shifts some of the accents. If it is certainly wrong to say that he abandons it,[53] it is still the case that he seems to refuse the terms of its most explicitly temporal interpretation. Reflecting on memory, Plotinus writes: "[M]emory, in the current sense, cannot be attributed to the Soul in connexion with the ideas inherent in its essence: these it holds not as a memory but as a possession . . . the Ancients . . . ascribe memory, and 'Recollection,' to souls bringing into outward manifestation the ideas they possess: we see at once that the memory here indicated is another kind; it is a memory outside of time."[54] Recollection of the truth, as actualization of what we virtually and naturally possess, thus is not to be confused with the debate over memory in the strict sense. There, it could have no past whatsoever. In another treatise, Plotinus envisions recollection as a means to go from time to eternity.[55] In this respect, he therefore abandons reflection on the absolute past, in favor of a conception of recol-

[52] I. Kant, "Über eine Entdeckung nach der alle neue Kritik der reinen Vernunft durch eine ältere entberlich gemacht werden soll," in *Werke,* vol. 3, p. 339 (*Akademie Textausgabe,* vol. 8, pp. 221–223).

[53] Among those who think otherwise is P. Merlan, in *The Cambridge History of Later Greek and Early Medieval Philosophy* (Cambridge: Cambridge University Press, 1970), p. 56: "As to anamnesis, Plotinus, in favor of the doctrine of the unconscious, virtually denies it." Yet Plotinus appeals to it frequently. Cf., e.g., *Enneads* I, 8, 15, pp. 69–70; II, 9, 16, pp. 127–129; III, 5, 1, pp. 174–176; etc.

[54] Plotinus, *Enneads* IV, 3, 25, pp. 278–279.

[55] Plotinus, *Enneads* III, 7, 1, pp. 213–214.

lection close to the one advanced by Leibniz. The most decisive basis for this abandon is a thesis proper to Plotinus that Proclus would frequently criticize, according to which the soul is not completely descendent into the sensible. Because it has something higher in it, it remains always close to spirit and the intelligible world, and is here only in delegated form. Forgetting would thus never affect it completely: the summit of the soul does not forget—never forgets—the truth and is not even exposed to the possibility of forgetting it. The path of recollection follows a line leading toward the self, toward what in us and of us that remains always intact, unaltered, and inalterable, and that we forget without losing it. There would thus be a return here to the origin, and an origin that one has never properly left—rather than a gathering, without return, of the truth given and withdrawn in forgetting.

Is this then to say that the thought of forgetting loses its centrality and force? More than a matter of forgetting the Ideas, it is for Plotinus henceforth directly a matter of forgetting the self. The forgetting of the origin is immediately a forgetting of self, and the will to be oneself opens, in separating us from the origin, to the most complete misunderstanding of the self. One of Plotinus's major treatises begins with the question: "What can it be that has brought the souls to forget the Father, God, and, though parts of the Divine and entirely of that world, to ignore at once themselves and It?"[56] Forgetting is consummated of the distance and "apostasy" of souls: a distance which suppresses itself as distance, which no longer knows what it is distant from and has renounced, which no longer relates to the lost origin, even and above all as lost. This forgetting of self and of the origin forms an active and positive misunderstanding which becomes the principle of all that makes up the soul. In forgetting their descent, souls strike themselves with indignity and contempt without knowing it. "They misplace their respect, honoring everything more than themselves." Everything becomes the subject of astonishment to the soul no longer astonished at it-

[56] Plotinus, *Enneads* V, 1, 1, pp. 347–348. The citations that follow are taken from this same chapter.

self. The indignity of the soul is not, in reality, marked by expressed thoughts of abasement, but by its abandon to the world. It is one and the same thing to say that the soul abases itself and that it elevates the things of the world that excite its desire. "Admiring pursuit of an external thing is, for the being who admires it and pursues it, a confession of inferiority." Plotinus illuminates a conception of the self as worked by worldly desire. To call "forgetting" the ignorance in which the soul thus finds itself, is to think this ignorance otherwise than as a simple absence of knowledge: as a positive form of being in the world and with oneself, it is that which one must break from in order to accede to philosophy. "To teach or recall the soul to its race and its honor"—for Plotinus, this is the primary task. All research must take the form above all of dis-covering, of lifting those who do seek and will seek away from forgetting. To seek what this is in truth, it is first necessary for one to regain oneself. And understanding oneself comes from a relation to self and a recollection of self. Like Plato, Plotinus envisages recollection as the condition for research, as what alone opens it in its proper place. But in making the self the primary object of this recollection, he nonetheless transforms its meaning.

The Plotinian thought of the beautiful confirms this new inflection. Plato's *Phaedrus*, following the erotic path of recollection, accords to beauty a unique force for making us overcome the forgetting of the Ideas. Plotinus maintains this favor for the beautiful but, in conformity with his reconsideration of anamnesis, invites us to discover the beauty of our soul. It is in becoming beautiful ourselves that we truly see beauty. The interiority of beauty gives itself truly to be seen only in ourselves, and for Plotinus recollection is indeed what Hegel will say it is: *Erinnerung, Insichgehen*. To recollect the beautiful is to become beautiful oneself, to become one's own vision of the beautiful and what it sees. How to see the beauty of the soul? "Draw back into yourself and look."[57] Those who seek beauty without having discovered their own seek with wretchedness and in wretchedness, and they will not be able to find it thus. "This is why," says

[57] Plotinus, *Enneads* I, 6, 9, p. 54.

the treatise on intelligible beauty, "such matters are not spoken of to everyone; you, if you are conscious of beauty within, remember."[58] Recollection is not a form of memory that would be opposed to the forgetting of some past. It is the discovery of being a self in its integrity, the tearing of a veil of misunderstanding and contempt. First is the forgetting, but this forgetting does not reduce to an event such as that of our birth. It renews itself in each circumstance where we misunderstand ourselves and mislead ourselves in pursuing what is less than ourselves, when elevating something, by our desire, to the status of what alone can fulfill and satisfy us, thus as something superior to us.

At first glance, it may seem that this thought of recollection leaves no room for a meditation on the immemorial as such. However, Plotinus evokes it with singular intensity in one page where he distinguishes our relation to the Good and our relation to the Beautiful. The modalities of our desire for the two would be radically different, and this difference would bring to light what there is there of the immemorial. The forgetting by which everything begins is no longer the forgetting of Ideas. Plotinus writes: "Certain people, we must keep in mind, have forgotten that to which their longing and their effort are pointed: for all that exists desires and aspires toward it by natural necessity, as if sensing that without it they cannot be."[59] The ensuing lines show that what there will be of the Good here, is opposed to the Beautiful with regard to their respective manifestations. Forgetting, as always already accomplished, perfect forgetting or forgetting perfectly what we desire, is not for all that the forgetting of desire, not its loss, and not its abolition. The evocation of the temporal extension of desire[60] clearly signifies: we never cease to desire what we have always already lost. We will desire it without either seeing or knowing what it is that we desire. Do those of us who lack this desire in fact lack it doubly? Is there a lack in the lack itself, a blind thrust *(élan)* founded on

[58] Plotinus, *Enneads* V, 8, 2, p. 413.

[59] Plotinus, *Enneads* V, 5, 12, pp. 402–404. The citations that follow are taken from the same location.

[60] Marcilio Ficino translates: *ab initio in hunc usque diem.*

the initial loss of what we still lack? With profundity, Plotinus sees there, on the contrary, a singular and unsubstitutable modality of presence, a presence in the forgetting itself—*the withdrawal of the immemorial is presence,* which can be characterized in no other way than precisely as the Good.

Only the Good could thus be forgotten without being lost. This would explain the prudence of the second phrase cited: what we have always already forgotten and yet never cease to desire, what we do not know of our desire, we feel by presentiment, says Plotinus, borrowing from the vocabulary of prophecy.[61] The obscurity of desire feels without seeing or anticipating what it has forgotten in advance. Contraction in the immemorial is presence, for the immemorial anticipates us, comes out to our initiative. But is it truly this that we divine? The fact that it is felt as that without which we cannot be, shows that in desiring it we tend not toward what would not yet be, but rather toward what has already come. Our desire for the Good supposes that the Good has already been given as the condition of our being. The desire for what founds us has already received the force of desiring, and in a sense it has already received everything that it could ever desire, and this is why it desires. The immemorial that is always already forgotten and always already there, is always still there—present in its contraction and by its very contraction. This contraction is not absence of presence, but excess of presence, excessive presence that we lack, inordinate presence for which no present could suffice.

The *already* of presence is said in several senses, and the *already* of beauty is distinguished profoundly from the *already* of the Good. "The perception of Beauty and the awe and stirring of love of it are for those already in some degree knowing and awakened." The beautiful claims an already mine—an awakening and a knowing that are mine—which anticipates and

[61] *Apomemonteumena.* Ficino translates: *quasi quae vaticinentur.* [Chrétien's word "pressentir" is commonly translated as "foreboding" or, as I have chosen, "presentiment." Appealing to Latin, one might venture Aquinas's *praegustatio,* or "foretaste." In any case, as the next lines of the text make clear, Plotinus's sense of this word avoids any suggestion of advance sight or grasp. Trans.]

appropriates its disturbing manifestation. For Plotinus, it will come only if I wait for it and keep my eyes open for it, and the very surprise it occasions supposes that I let myself be surprised. It is not necessary to sleep or close one's eyes. But to remain vigilant, one must wait for something, anticipate and foresee it in one or another manner, even if it is not I who would make it come. To let the beautiful be and to let it come is already, in every sense, to belong to it. The Good, for its part, supposes nothing; it does not need our foresight or foreknowledge. It has already come in our very forgetting. To the vigilance of those who see the beautiful, Plotinus opposes the presence of the Good to even those who sleep. "The Good, as possessed long since and setting up a connatural tendency, is present even to sleepers." The turn of phrase employed here by Plotinus, *paron eis*, indicates, according to de Bailly's Greek-French dictionary, "the idea of an anterior movement," which it paraphrases thus: "to have come and been found present."[62] With respect to the Good, Plotinus is not so much a thinker of "total presence" as a thinker of immemorial presence, which is an entirely different thing. It will be a matter here of another already, another bygone past: not the bygone past of another time, but one that is other than any and every time.

According to this meditation by Plotinus, Beauty is properly what comes into presence and to my own presence: Beauty is encountered. The fact that the Good is always present does not confirm the primacy of presence and of the present, but exceeds all presence in advance, according to an absolute past, a bygone past. "It brings no wonder (as does the Beautiful) when [some people] see it at a certain moment *(pote),*" Plotinus goes on, "since it is always with them, and is no occasional recollection *(oupote hè anamnèsis).*" The presence of the Good forms a oneness with us, a being united with us, the immemorial character of which forbids all that would belong to the order of an encounter, with its double movement of anticipation and its mutual envelopment. This presence does not signify the pure

[62] From *pareimi.* Liddell and Scott's Greek-English dictionary says "to have arrived at."

actuality of the non-temporal for us, since the Good is *already* there for us. In what sense? An earlier chapter of the same Tractate says of the Good, with a formula admirable in its precision, "it has come as not coming."[63] No one—not even at the summit of being—has ever assisted at the advent of the Good. The Good has come without witness. The past of its coming is absolutely immemorial; it has never been present and will never be re-presented, nor will it ever be recaptured by any recollection. This past is forgotten by a forgetting anterior to all memory, and which can only found all memory and all recollection of what is not the Good itself. There can be neither simultaneity nor coincidence with it. In effect, it lets itself be seen as "something present before all else, before the Intellect itself."[64] Always already there, always already come, the Good is that which forever escapes all anamnesis. Yet this does not express a negative trait that would render it unthinkable, but rigorously describes, in distinguishing it from the Beautiful, its mode of presence in the contraction of the immemorial. This contraction does not succeed to an appearance, does not slip away from what would have been given first: we have always already received the Good in its withdrawal, even before being and in order to be. This is why the Good is that which one does not apperceive. "The more primal appetite not patent to sense, our movement towards our good, gives witness that the Good is earlier than Beauty, and anterior to it."[65] The immemorial of the Good leaves in us a mark that is itself immemorial, the desire that we have for it. This is a mark without remark, a forgotten presence, but always already at work. The Good is the "older *(presbuteron)*—not in time, but by degree of reality, and it has the higher and anterior power." The gentleness, delicacy, the very goodness of the Good are nothing other than its imme-

[63] Plotinus, *Enneads* V, 5, 8, p. 399. *Elthén hôs ouk elthôn.* [The English translation has: "it is coming without approach." Trans.]

[64] Ibid. [The English translation has: "something present before all else, before the Intellect itself made any movement." Trans.] The passive perfect *ôphthè* that Plotinus uses here also plays an important role in Christian scripture.

[65] Plotinus, *Enneads* V, 5, 12, pp. 402–404, here as well as for the following citations.

morial anticipation. Because it never comes, because it has always already come, because there is in it—by reason of this very past—neither advent nor event, "when one wishes for it, it is already present to us." Not that it comes at our call: our desire, itself immemorial, and older in us than ourselves, is already bound up with it and bound to it. Directing ourselves toward it makes us discover that we are already in it. The Good that sends all being and all gift, the Good that promises all, has already kept its promise and is itself, for Plotinus, beyond being. But it is beyond being in all being: it is in this that it would not entail any recollection. However, the negation of all anamnesis of the good does not mean that Plotinus renounces the thought of the immemorial. The ancientness of the Good does not come to the present by recollection. The *other past* is consistent with an *other forgetting*, according to a mode different than the one that Plato himself had formulated.

This correlation between the beyond being and the non-rememberable is rediscovered, in what may seem an identical manner, in the thought of Emmanuel Levinas. And after all, can there be a thought of the beyond being that is not in some way Platonic? The very project owes its title to Plato, who foresees the horizon of everything that one calls "neo-Platonism," *épékéina tès ousias.*[66] Levinas's *Otherwise than Being or Beyond Essence* is a Platonic title par excellence. And there is certainly something not yet worked out in the proximity to a certain Platonism of attempts to overcome metaphysics, of which Platonism is, moreover, thought to be the foundation. For Levinas, to interrogate the beyond being is to turn toward "a diachrony refractory to all synchronization, a transcending diachrony," toward "a past more ancient than any representable origin, a pre-original and anarchic passed," toward a past "that bypasses the present, the pluperfect past," "immemorial, unrepresentable, invisible." "Irrecuperable by reminiscence . . . by reason of its incommensurability with the present," such a past, says Levinas, "shows itself in the present of obedience, without being recalled there, without coming there from memory."[67]

[66] *Republic* VI, 509b.

[67] Levinas, op. cit., pp. 9, 11, 13.

This lost time, lost in advance, "the immemorial past that has not crossed the present,"[68] is consistent with what binds me, before any consent, to the other *(l'autre).* It is one with the responsibility without measure that constitutes me in the accusative.[69] The face of the other person *(d'autrui)* has always already called to me and rendered me responsible; the immemorial goes together with the fact that this command is unforgettable. This ethical dimension separates such a thinking from that of Plotinus, for whom ethics would not be the most high but would lead toward the most high, toward the first principle. However, this is not without some tension.

In the religious tradition, divine commandments do not, in fact, share in the immemorial and a past other than all memory: they come under a sacred history of which they constitute a major and founding event, by their givenness as well as by their reception. Sacred history is that which must always be remembered, and in cult and prayer form its perpetual anamnesis—because it is present, because it continues, and because the present instant inscribes itself there. To think the call of the Good as the law and commandment of God: is this to engage in a thought of the immemorial, or to pull away from it? To say that ethics breaks the subject's contemporaneity with itself is not yet to say how it does so—either according to the sacred history that is always remembered and thus capable of being remembered, where I can and must remember and remind myself of the others in it but who were not present to us, or according to an immemorial without history that reaches me in my very constitution as a subject and from the encounter with another person always prior to my every project. This is the site of a tension that Levinas does not elucidate.

It remains the case that in his own fashion, and because he renders it consistent with a philosophy of subjectivity whose "diachrony" no longer appears as anything but an interior constitutive wound, Levinas resumes the Platonic thought of a lost time

[68] Ibid., p. 58.

[69] Cf. our study, "La dette et l'élection," in M. Abensour and C. Chalier, eds., *Cahiers de l'Herne; Emmanuel Levinas* (Paris: L'Herne, 1991).

which would never be regained as such, and which alone sends us and destines us, which alone gives us being into the future. This immemorial of the sending, where what sends us in advance of us, is a loss that founds the gift. Such a forgetting before forgetting is profoundly different than the forgetting of self that Heidegger discusses, though it is true that the latter also has the sense of an initial forgetting. Both in *Being and Time* and in his course on the *Basic Problems of Phenomenology,* Heidegger deploys a positive thought of forgetting. This is not nothing, for it could lead back to a loss or privation of memory.[70] "This is a peculiar, positively ecstatic modality of temporality."[71] What comes first is forgetting, in so far as it forms the condition of the possibility of memory in the usual sense. "Remembering is possible only on the basis of forgetting, *and not vice versa.*"[72] And this first forgetting is forgetting of self as "flight before ownmost having-been." This having-been *(Gewesenheit),* as a mode of being, must not be confused with the "vulgar conception of the past" *(Vergangenheit)* and must not be determined on its basis. Only the existent can have been. Now, "forgetting is an elementary mode of temporality in which we *are* primarily and for the most part our own having-been."[73]

Such a forgetting of self does not have memory by contrast; it does not efface but flees, and thus relates itself to the very thing it flees. It makes us flee toward that which preoccupies us. The measure of this relinquishment of self is all that it makes us grasp. And "it is only on the basis of this originary forgottenness *(ursprünglichen Vergessenheit)* that belongs to factical Dasein, that there opens the possibility of retaining something toward which one was just now expecting,"[74] as well as the possibility of not retaining it, thus of forgetting it in the usual sense which, however, is shown here to be only a secondary and de-

[70] The citations that follow are taken from M. Heidegger, *Being and Time,* trans. E. Robinson and J. Macquarrie (London: SCM Press, 1962), § 68, pp. 387–389, and M. Heidegger, *Basic Problems of Phenomenology,* trans. A. Hofstadter (Bloomington: Indiana University Press, 1988), pp. 289–290.

[71] Heidegger, *Basic Problems of Phenomenology,* p. 290.

[72] Heidegger, *Being and Time,* p. 389. [Translation modified. Trans.]

[73] Heidegger, *Basic Problems of Phenomenology,* p. 290.

[74] Ibid., p. 290. [Translation modified. Trans.]

rived sense. What is opposed here to the first forgetting is not memory as capacity for retention, but what Heidegger calls repetition, *Wiederholung.*[75] Founded in the future, this repetition does not at all reproduce a past, does not imitate it or conform itself to it, but renews existence by *recalling* its possibilities. It has nothing in common with remembering in the usual sense, and it does not make any memory return. Thus understood, repetition can without doubt truly forget, or forget in truth, and in such a fashion that this forgetting is neither a forgetting of self, nor a returning of self to things. For forgetting first of all where we are, far from lightening and delivering us, enslaves and imprisons us in handing us over to blind possibilities. It overcomes nothing at all. This loss into inauthenticity is that in which being-there would, at each instant, grasp itself anew—it would therefore in reality grasp itself and truly know itself only in re-grasping itself—but this loss does not form its destining any more than it puts in play the immemorial, or the other past. If this (Heideggerian) forgetting is first, it would not be according to the sense of the forgetting taken up in earlier discussions. The fact remains that there is here a close relation between forgetting and care.

It is essential to the Platonic reflection on forgetting that the forgetful life is not the uncaring life but rather the life weighted with concern. The myth of the river of forgetting, of Lèthè, whose waters the souls of hell drink before incarnating or reincarnating, while it does make the depth of forgetting the very mark of the depth of the fall and corruption, nevertheless it confers a positive sense on forgetting.[76] The soul takes forgetting into itself, it satisfies itself there, fills itself; forgetting is not lightening, but weighting oneself down.[77] Far from being an absence, forgetting seeks the presence of what keeps the truth at a distance, or covers it up. Hence does it go with our faults and at the same time their punishment. For though our relation to the truth is not completely abolished, it is alienated and al-

---

[75] Heidegger, *Being and Time,* § 74, pp. 436–438.

[76] Cf. Proclus, *De malorum subsistentia,* 21, ed. and trans. D. Isaac (Paris: Les Belles lettres, 1982), pp. 55–56.

[77] Cf. *Phaedrus* 248c.

tered. Forgetting produces an ignorance of self that is positive. Thought mythically to be anterior to birth, this forgetting became, for the Platonists, the very title of our presence to the sensible, which confirms its positivity. For Plotinus, the true river Lèthè is the body itself. "The moving and *fluid* nature of the body must be the cause of forgetting and not of memory: and it is thus that one might interpret the river Lèthè."[78] Proclus goes further, making it the whole of the sensible world: "*River* designates not only the human body, but also the entire created world that surrounds us from outside, due to the impetuous unbalanced flux in it. And at any rate, in the *Republic* Plato has referred to the entire nature of the created world as 'river of Forgetting.' "[79] We thus never cease to drink of the water of the river of forgetting. Here, "forgetting" is the most proper name of our earthly condition, its restlessness, and its impermanence. The presence in us of ideas and reasons contemplated before our incarnation is not a force purely opposed to forgetting. For, paradoxically, if forgetting is an evil, be it however a necessary one bound up with the incarnation of the soul, for Proclus the greatest of evils—that is to say, the ignorance of ignorance, or the forgetting of forgetting—is stimulated not by forgetting itself, and not by the powers of the sensible, but by what of the truth subsists in us. Hence does he write in his commentary on Plato's *First Alcibiades:* "We do not know ourselves, because we are captive of the forgetting that belongs to the world of generation and sidetracked by the trouble stimulated by the irrational forms of life, and, by the innate notions *(logoi)* present according to our being, we imagine ourselves to know many things of which, in reality, we are ignorant."[80] This same thought is developed with vigor during the entire course of the commentary. In incarnating, souls receive forgetting, "and from the fact that the reasons of things are in them, as it were, palpitat-

[78] Plotinus, *Enneads* IV, 3, 26, p. 281. [Translation substantially modified. Trans.]

[79] Proclus, *Commentaire sur le Timée,* vol. 5, trans. A Festugière (Paris: Les Belles lettres, 1968), pp. 207–208.

[80] Proclus, *Sur le Premier Alcibiade de Platon,* vol. 1, trans. A. Segonds (Paris: Les Belles lettres, 1968), p. 5.

ing, they have thoughts about those things, but since they are subject to the filter of forgetting, these souls are incapable of articulating their own thoughts and delivering them to science. They bear the ideas in themselves and it is only with great difficulty that they can express them or, in a manner of speaking, exude them; yet souls thus acquire a double ignorance, for they believe they know on the basis of the ideas but are in fact in ignorance due to forgetting them."[81] This double ignorance marks the deepest fall, the imprisonment par excellence, since it prohibits even the search for truth and paralyzes our desire. It is from this that philosophy must first and foremost deliver us. Now, this same fall and imprisonment is itself provoked by that which renders philosophy and science possible: the inadmissibility of our relation to truth, or the presence in us of that which we would like to recover by recollection. The pre-possession—obscure, latent, unarticulated—of truth is that which throws us into the illusion of knowing. That which remains in a sense outside the reach of forgetting, the unforgettable character of what in essence belongs to us, forms what can make us forget supremely and fall into the worst sort of illusion. The pre-possession of science is taken for science: here would be ignorance at its limit.

Inversely, if the forgetting bound to sensible life makes us flee truth and turns us away from it, it never does so without also turning us toward the world. Forgetting and care cannot be separated. "It is born in us," writes Proclus, "to forget sometimes one thing and sometimes another, and in such a way are borne to us the things by which we find ourselves to be, and in such a way we also fall into forgetting all the things, such as they are, that we do not bring into range due to idleness and want of effort."[82] Forgetting is completely contrary to vacancy, for in each instance it throws us and opens us to preoccupation with what lies before us. Proclus does not view this forgetful preoccupation, or this careful forgetting, solely as a mode of decline.

---

[81] Ibid., vol. 2, p. 249.

[82] Proclus, *Commentaire sur la République*, vol. 3, trans. Festugière, pp. 306–307.

There is in this forgetting of the intelligible also something providential, where it reveals itself as authentically founding. Forgetting is at once distress and the way out of distress. "What soul," asks Proclus, "if it maintained the memory of things over there [before and beyond this world], would accept care for the body and generation? But forgetting life there, of the easy existence there, makes us to take upon ourselves the care of what lies before our eyes. Hence have there appeared the skills necessary for life, and hence have the sciences penetrated the intelligence and divinity of this place here, in a manner giving reason to the generation deprived of reason and adorning the place of evils with a thousand diverse goods."[83] Forgetting is thus providential, and for Proclus there exists a chasm between the respective functions of forgetting and of the presence in us of ideas: the former can be the origin of developments among people of arts and sciences, whereas the latter can enclose us in illusion.

Just the same, recollection dissociates us from all nostalgia. When it takes place, it represents an act of forgetting essentially consistent with our condition: it does not aim at anything that it has already done. If recollection is for Proclus the passage from an understanding of the inarticulate to articulation,[84] the forgetting by which the reasons that are in us are ungraspable by us is also what requires us, by prohibiting every repetition and any move behind, to articulate them. The silent word of our soul must utter itself. It is thus alone that we grasp it. Even if the Platonic thought of forgetting renders it consistent with a fall of the soul, still it recognizes a positivity there and makes it a mode of our being in the world, a structure of our life whose deployment it studies. It is this that furnishes Kierkegaard with a guiding thread leading straight to the arguments that, in his *Philosophical Fragments,* develop the possibility of Christian revelation as the other of Platonic recollection. But by what

[83] Ibid. [As will be clear from the previous reference to "generation," Proclus here intends the domain of growth and decay and thus, more generally, of earthly existence. Trans.]

[84] Proclus, *Sur le Premier Alcibiade,* vol. 2, trans. Segonds, pp. 250–251.

understanding? For Kierkegaard, if the truth is always in myself, the one who makes me, through maeiutics, discover and rediscover it, is only the concrete occasion for this. He will have been nothing but an occasion that immediately retires, leaving me to myself, according to a process that would deny all importance to the *instant* of discovery. If recollection makes me recapture the immemorial truth through the hidden forgetting, this does not withdraw the very act of recollection from time. Discovering the immemorial can be unforgettable. Proclus writes: "Thus, I know of the idea *(eidos)* of the circle that I have learned its definition at this or that time, of the idea of justice its definition at some other time, and thus for each of the beings of which we have knowledge in act."[85] Recollection does not volatilize time. Forgetting and recollection, in the Platonic senses, amount to a thought of the temporality of knowledge.

Across these diverse possibilities and transformations, Platonic thought thus supposes a forgetting that is first and founding. Such a forgetting, itself one with our human condition, does not come from an already constituted memory, and could not be defined as its failure. It precedes and renders possible our authentic memory of the truth, which is recollection. This latter is not to be considered a step back behind, and it does not go back to some past, does not render any past present: it makes us catch hold of ourselves from out of the immemorial truth. Forgetting is the dimension according to which being sends us, calls to us, and promises us, throws us forward. Our initial lag behind the truth will never be filled or made up, and recollection could never be transformed into pure and simple memory. There is thus indeed a loss that founds us, and this loss only gives, and gives us. Access to the truth takes place only according to forgetting, overcome but not abolished, and thus the parousia of the truth is for us never either plenitude or coincidence. In the *Phaedo,* Plato emphasizes that the kinship of the soul with the ideas is not at all an identity. The reduction of such an anteriority to the *a priori* overlooks what is most

[85] Ibid.

profound about recollection, and what is most pregnant with the future.

Forgetting is the measure of the excess of the Good over us. It is all the more deserving of reflection that, as the next chapter will show, there is nothing more difficult to think than loss, and that the most constant trait of philosophers of forgetting consists in showing that no forgetting is irreparable, whereas everything is in some manner unforgettable. The excessive presence of the Good can reach us only in waiting for us. It only wounds us through its radical past as through its radical future, neither of the two being a deferred presence, an ancient present and a future present. In a style that is never more beautiful than when it moves only with some awkwardness, Ernest Hello writes: "The thing that seeks us sometimes finds us during the forgetting."[86] According to him, forgetting is in play in our lives in the forms of sleep, laughter, and intoxication. But what seeks us from eternity also seeks us through forgetting, across forgetting, and without return, thus destining us. And there is therefore no "during the forgetting," but only a "since forgetting," for recollection renders forgetting unforgettable, and reveals what in it looks upon us. It is thus that Maurice Blanchot evokes "the present which . . . would make forgetting: the free presence of every present," "which did not let itself wait in expectation, which did not let itself forget in forgetting,"[87] forgetting as "latent gift."[88]

One representative of the failure to appreciate this latent gift is the thought of Philo of Alexandria, who completely reverses the respective import of memory and reminiscence in Platonism. Thus, in the *Legum allegoriae,* among many other passages testifying to this opposition, he writes: in the soul, God has created in the soul two extremely necessary natural functions, "memory and recollection *(mnèmè te kai anamnèsis).* Memory is superior, recollection inferior. For while the former keeps apprehensions that are always fresh and clear, so that it does

[86] E. Hello, *Paroles de Dieu. Réflexions sur quelques textes sacrés* (Paris: n.p., 1877), p. 4.

[87] M. Blanchot, *L'attente oubli* (Paris: Gallimard, 1962), p. 103.

[88] Ibid., p. 87.

not fall due to ignorance, recollection is, in all cases, preceded by forgetting, being mutilated and blind."[89] Nevertheless, for Philo recollection is anterior to memory,[90] for we are exposed first of all to forgetting, and memory comes only later: their succession is the inverse of their dignity. This inferiority of recollection comes from its solidarity with forgetting, but this latter is therefore plainly though in wholly different fashion [than in Platonism].

The Platonic thought privileged here is certainly not the only one, even if it is the first, to have meditated on the immemorial. In *The Ages of the World,* Schelling has also undertaken this exercise, attempting to think that which would already be *presupposed* in every posing, that which, before one reflects or even ventures to do so, is already there, and has occupied the place of unconditionality from that deep anteriority so that we might come into being[91]—just as he has also thought a first past and an absolute future. But the Platonic project is more decisive, in that it coincides with the foundation of metaphysics, and may already exceed it. Just as modern interpretations of Plato forget forgetting, so theories of forgetting constitute its perpetual negation. Is memory the perpetual memorial of what exceeds us, founded on a first forgetting that sends us, or the place of a parousia without fault?

---

[89] Philo of Alexandria, *Legum allegoriae,* III, 91. *Philo of Alexandria,* vol. 1, trans. F. H. Colson and G. H. Whitaker (Cambridge: Harvard/Loeb, 1929), p. 363. [The Loeb translations of Philo are cited throughout this book, but frequently modified. Trans.]

[90] Ibid., III, 92; 1:363.

[91] Cf. F. W. J. Schelling, *The Ages of the World,* trans. J. Wirth (Albany: SUNY Press, 2000), pp. 78f.

2

The Reserve of Forgetting

Rien n'est perdu de ce qui m'est soustrait.
(Nothing is lost of what escapes me.)

THIS PHRASE from André du Bouchet[1] goes past the limits of its own situation to bring out a paradox common to all thoughts of forgetting. The fact that a memory has escaped us, and that we could not recover and make use of it: this we experience each day, and refer to as "forgetting." But does this withdrawal of a memory signify loss? Does the non-availability of a memory demonstrate that it has been destroyed and lost, in which case forgetting would be the adverse and contrary power of memory, or does this only signify that such a memory, presently outside our reach, is secret, hidden, and held in reserve, in which case forgetting would only be another name for memory, as its latent treasury, its virtual richness, and one of its essential modes? This second possibility dominates the history of thought, and this is why the words of André du Bouchet can serve as the legend for many reflections on forgetting.

Yet forgetting seems at first glance to be one of the most intimate and vivid events of loss. What in myself is lost, what is erased and disappears there—if there is such a thing—is lost much more profoundly than any being in the world, which is always only mislaid or displaced, thus lost in the sense of not being there where I seek it. If my memory can lose something, it does so without remainder, since what it loses does not and could not have presence except through my remembering. Is

[1] A. du Bouchet, *Ici en deux* (Paris: Mercure, 1986), no pagination. A first version of this chapter made up the text of a conference given at the Ecole normale supérieure in May 1989 in a seminar on phenomenology directed by J.-F. Courtine.

the inflection of cherished voices of those who have died—voices whose diaeresis momentarily disrupts the poet's voice[2]—completely lost even while I continue to hear their resonance at the bottom of my throat? And is the light in their vanished faces extinguished even while its distant rays still reach us, scintillating in the night of our closed eyes? Can one truly lose in any other way than by forgetting, where we no longer retain even the fact of having lost and where we no longer even mourn the loss? If forgetting signifies loss, it tears us from ourselves and mutilates us in our interiority, for to lose something in oneself is also, necessarily, to lose something of oneself. This loss of self despite oneself is distinguished from all sacrifice and every renunciation, unless it is possible for there to be a sacrifice that sacrifices itself and a renunciation that renounces itself. For the loss that occurs through forgetting this or that aspect of my past is given first of all as powerlessness, as loss of power to relate and bear presence. This latter trait seems to deepen and, as it were, seal the meaning of loss, since I will have lost not only what happened or what I did, but a dimension of what I am and can do. It is this, however, that opens a gap between two conceptions of forgetting, and this gap will permit one to deny that forgetting is indeed loss. It will permit one to abolish its possibility, and to erase the principle of erasure from which forgetting takes its name—it will permit one, perhaps, to forget the forgetting.

Yet this powerlessness to remember which currently withholds the object of remembrance from me cannot be taken for proof of radical loss, since we never cease, through the whole of our life, to recover memories that had escaped from us only provisionally or temporarily. What would guarantee, in a specific case, that this powerlessness could not one day be overcome? There is no lack of testimony to the frequently unexpected return of a past that was previously supposed lost from memory. Hence does W. H. Hudson write, at the beginning of a book relating memories of his childhood in Argentina,

---

[2] P. Verlaine, "Mon rêve familier," in *Poëmes saturniens* (Paris: Gallimard, 1973).

that "it is easy to delude oneself and believe that some facts of one's life that one remembers and discerns best are precisely the most important, and have, for that reason, survived in memory, whereas the rest have been erased forever." As his entire book shows, this loss is only an illusion, born of a circumstance in which it was "suddenly revealed, and as if miraculously, that nothing is abolished."[3] Who has not known such a miracle? Can what is written and traced in us ever be truly wiped away, or are we, in moments of forgetfulness, merely in the impossibility of rediscovering or deciphering some such inscription? Can anything that enters the vast spaces and ample palace of memory of which Augustine writes[4] ever be destroyed, or does it only disappear temporarily, thus becoming inaccessible in fact, even while remaining there? Can what slips away from me ever be lost? Or is it only in retreat? If it is to be the latter, then forgetting is nothing other than the reserve of memory, the treasury from which memory can ceaselessly draw without possibility of diminishing it, and without possibility of us using up the least part of it. Even the most impoverished among us always enjoy this treasure.

The Augustinian images could certainly be critiqued, and they appear to amount to constructions of a spiritual mythology insofar as they seem to transform memories into subsistent beings in us, independent of us and of our acts. But when the same thinkers, to whom such constructions are by their design the most foreign, themselves follow the constitutive principle that admits at the meaning of loss only non-availability and impossibility of recovery, they, too, leave intact what there is to recover. In effect, nothing would ever be erased, but I would not always be able to read. This capacity is perhaps by all rights surmountable in any instance. Its sheer intermittence tends to prove this, since every day seems to include moments remembering what was still held in forgetting only the day before, just as each day we also forget what was still easily remembered a

[3] W. H. Hudson, *Far Away and Long Ago. A History of My Early Life (Wild Places)* (New York: Lyons Press, 1997), p. 7.

[4] Augustine, *Confessions* X, viii, 12 and X, xvii, 26, trans. H. Chadwick (Oxford: Oxford University Press, 1991), respectively pp. 185–186 and 194–195.

day ago. The greatest part of our past does not present itself immediately to our memory, but requires, in order to be remembered, an effort, a search, a more or less rigorous progression in which Aristotle, before many others, detected certain laws.[5] What does this say, if not that this past must be drawn out from forgetting? The very experience of forgetting is thus precisely the proof that nothing is truly lost, if it is indeed capable of becoming some mislaid object that one rediscovers, and at the instant in which one expects it the least.

There is thus much more support than one might believe for the following affirmation made in Nietzsche's *Daybreak:* "It has not yet been proved that there is any such thing as forgetting; all we know is that the act of recollection does not lie in our power."[6] The word *forgetting,* Nietzsche continues, thus marks a weak spot in our power which for its part thereby endows us with one more faculty—that of forgetting. Nietzsche makes this transformation the occasion for an interrogation of other pretended faculties. The fact that one could not remember does not prove that one could forget, and that something escapes me does not prove that I could lose something. That which is given as a limit of our power to remember, we attribute to another faculty—that of forgetting—displaying the same illusory pride that Nietzsche denounces in neighboring aphorisms. The inaccessibility of a memory is evident, but what is not yet proven is that it could be lost. This consequence does not follow from what we believe possible or impossible for our being. Far from going together with the recognition of our limits, speaking of a power to forget is still a presumption. Does it suffice to oppose this in the manner of Maurice Blanchot, citing the same words from Nietzsche: "Exactly: unproven, improbable, forgetfulness, vigilance that ever awakens us"?[7] This purely rhetorical reversal of the impossibility of proving forgetting into an impossible for-

---

[5] Aristotle, *De memoria et reminiscentia,* II, in *Parva naturalia.*

[6] F. Nietzsche, *Daybreak*, Bk. II, § 126, trans. R. J. Hollingdale (Cambridge: Cambridge University Press, 1983), p. 126. Cf. M. Heidegger, *Zollikoner Seminare* (Frankfurt: Klostermann, 1987), pp. 212–213.

[7] M. Blanchot, *The Writing of the Disaster,* trans. A. Smock (Lincoln: University of Nebraska Press, 1995), p. 105.

getting without proof, though nonetheless real, and whose improbability would be proven by the very absence of proof, does not at all help in reaching a better understanding of the questions stimulating by forgetting.

No more Augustinian than Nietzsche might be, and no closer to evoking the palace of memory, Paul Valéry, in many of the reflections on memory and forgetting recorded in his *Cahiers*, sharply distinguishes loss and escape. "Forgetting," he writes, "is the growing insensibility of the system *(appareil)* to put memory to work. I am inclined to think that remembering is indestructible in its power. But the act is rare."[8] Elsewhere, the affirmation is still plainer: "The Memory does not lose. Remembering is indelible. It is the path of remembering that loses."[9] It is from here that Valéry comes to wonder: "What if a memory can always be radically abolished, that is to say, if no circumstance could ever reanimate it?"[10] Beginning the moment when loss is denied, the question necessarily arises whether the withdrawal can be definitive, in which case for us it would count as loss. These assertions show quite well that for such analyses, nothing of what escapes me is lost. The appearance of loss is not to be mistaken for loss, and can even count as the contrary of loss. For would not the indelible memory to which we do not rediscover access—the memory that is forgotten while still a memory—remain intact, kept safe and in reserve, thus by a retreat which would also give it an inalterable freshness? Would not the forgotten memory also be the most promising memory, the memory richest in futurity?

Such a question shows that the distinction between loss and escape of a memory, between its complete erasure and its more or less temporary unavailability, makes possible a poetics of forgetting. Here, "poetics" is understood in the broad sense, indicating that forgetting, far from unmaking, makes, and far from destroying and decomposing, produces and creates. It is in denying a radical forgetting that both Nietzsche and Valéry open

[8] P. Valéry, *Cahiers*, vol. 1, (Paris: Gallimard, 1973), p. 1236. Valéry nonetheless also seems to admit a forgetting that is loss.

[9] Ibid., p. 1239.

[10] Ibid., p. 1240.

a space for the praise of the forgetting that crosses their thinking. What this praise sees in forgetting is not at all the negation or privation of memory, but rather its foundation and condition; it supports a poetics of memory with a poetics of forgetting. In this perspective, the beautiful title of a collection of poems by Jules Supervielle, *Oublieuse mémoire,* forgetful memory—which itself takes on a tragic sense, if *a thousand fleeing birds make but one that lands*—would not be oxymoronic, but pleonastic (the *pleon*, the surplus of memory): for it would be necessary for memory to be forgetful in order for it to be memory, and the forgetting would form what preserves it, what is most vital in its power. Yet there are different ways of conceiving this point, just as there are different ways of understanding that nothing is lost of what escapes me.

Nothing is lost can mean first of all that our past is preserved and conserved in us, that nothing can be destroyed—such are the retreat and latency where the past might be held in store for our conscious presence. According to this first conception, the total and integral conservation of the past, in us, can make of our memory a reserve without limit—thus limited not even by the consciousness that we had of the past when it was present. Memories would have a future that would not only be that of returning. Preserved in us, a small perception could deliver and explicate its meaning and its bearing afterwards, so that memory could sometimes be, as Valéry has said, a power of the first time. "Memory has frequently been utilized to perceive *for the first time* events so brief that direct perception has been almost nil and useless."[11] We could see again more than we have seen. Not only is nothing of what was present erased, but also nothing of what was not present in the present. This first conception can in some cases lead to a direct and express affirmation of an "exaltation of memory," to borrow, with Bergson, some terms from Leibniz. Natural or supernatural, this exaltation of memory would be the act in which we would recall in a unique present the totality of our past being. Whatever the case with this exaltation, it is clear that according to this conception

[11] Ibid., p. 1225.

all memory can by right be recovered, voluntarily or involuntarily, and that the integral conservation of our past, even if latent, is necessarily oriented towards a possible parousia, even if this must remain a simple teleological idea. But a past that would be integrally conserved but destined to remain forever inaccessible would only be a construct of reason.

Nothing is lost can also mean, according to a second conception, that everything of our past is conserved in as much as what of this past is truly ours, or what we have made ours, is saved forever. From this perspective, memory as power of assimilation, integration, and appropriation is one with forgetting as power of rejection, erasure, and expulsion. If all of the essential is preserved, and if only the essential is preserved, there is certainly loss, as distinct from what the previous definition asserts, but this loss does not deprive us of anything. On the contrary, it gives us truly to ourselves, in relieving us and freeing us of what of the past would remain a foreign and inassimilable body. This loss does not at all uproot us and forbids us nothing, but is only the expulsion by memory without which its inspiration would die out. The same also applies to the time evoked by Charles Péguy, in *Clio*, "when there were just enough lost documents (and consequently there were just enough documents remaining), which would guarantee that they were rightly lost, that is to say that it would be just those that it was necessary to lose which were lost."[12] To lose what one must lose is thus the condition for keeping what must be kept, which is thus to have lost truly nothing but gained everything. Relief *(délestage)* is not mourning. To this second conception of *nothing is lost* corresponds the majority of poetics of forgetting. If we forget in order to remember, and truly forget in order to remember in truth, then the praise of forgetting also sings of memory.

In either of these approaches, forgetfulness is necessarily memory so that my past is conserved in its integrity. Even if the comprehension of forgetting differs, it alone insures the integrity of memory. Forgetting and memory are not at all contradictory here, and their relations are not agonistic either in principle

[12] C. Péguy, *Clio* (Paris: Gallimard, 1948), p. 196.

or by right, even if this can appear to be so when it is a matter of a particular memory. Why? If one presupposes, as one would when adhering to the first conception, a complete conservation of our past that is both integral and accurate, then it must indeed be in us without being immediately present to us; it must be that it escapes and distances itself from our attention and our current consciousness. Saying that it remains entirely without any loss and saying that it cannot be entirely remembered are in fact two forms of the same assertion. It is self-evident that under the normal conditions of consciousness, it is impossible for me to remember in a same present moment everything that has ever occurred to me, and above all if I conserve it down to the finest detail. The integral presence of the past is thus identical to its latency, its indestructibility is simultaneously its being held in reserve, and it is preserved in being reserved; memory and forgetting coincide, if by forgetting one understands simply the retreat outside of present consciousness. According to the second conception, where the necessity of loss is admitted, the integrity and integrality of the past, far from coinciding, are excluded for memory. All keeping would come down to neither holding nor retaining anything, and a total, integral memory, instead of guaranteeing the integrity of the meaning of our life, would open on to nonsense and chaos. In order for the memory as such to be able to appear, it is necessary that certain aspects of the past be erased and disappear. Forgetting is thus defined and takes place in view of memory, just as appropriation supposes exclusion. Without forgetting, there would be nothing that I could remember.

Whether it is thought as the latency of memory, the holding in reserve of the past, or as expulsion of an inassimilable and meaningless past, forgetting beats in each instance as the very heart of memory. In the first case, our whole life is written, traced, or inscribed, and nothing is ever erased if it has been deposited in the archives of memory, which are also the archives of forgetting. In the second case, writing supposes that one erases what one need not write, with the erasures of forgetting giving memory its style and obliteration being what permits sending oneself one's past. To speak of forgetting is never anything but to speak of memory and its power, not because the one would refer to the other as to its contrary, but because forgetting is thus only another name for memory, and perhaps its most proper name.

Such thoughts abolish the difficulty of an access to forgetting. If forgetting belongs necessarily to my memory—whether as a holding in reserve that constitutes a treasury, or as an elimination of what does not have to be retained—it is an act that is properly mine, an act of which I am the origin. Why is its meaning concealed from me more than that of any other of my acts? If, on the other hand, forgetting can be a veritable loss, if I can be impassioned by forgetting, the very access to forgetting and the possibility of speaking of it become much more difficult. There is nothing futile in the aporiae taken up by Augustine concerning the memory of forgetting. To pronounce the name "memory" is to have the very thing present in memory. But how is this possible? How can one know forgetting itself? "How then is it present for me to remember when, if it is present I have no power of remembering?"[13] André du Bouchet also brings out this aporia when he writes: "Knowing—I forget. . . . (I would not speak of things I have not *effectively* forgotten)."[14] Such questions could not even be posed if forgetting, purely mine, is the condition of memory. What is it, and what does it cost when the possibility of loss is denied, when nothing is lost of what escapes me? Now is the proper moment to make a test of this by studying more precisely the two aforementioned conceptions of *nothing is lost.*

Bergson belongs among those who have affirmed with greatest force the impossibility of loss. As distinct from habit, the true memory "retains and ranges alongside each other all of our states and in the order in which they occur, leaving to each fact its place and consequently marking its date, truly moving it into the past."[15] In the depths of consciousness memories are kept

---

[13] Augustine, *Confessions* X, xvi, 24, trans. H. Chadwick, p. 193.

[14] A. du Bouchet, *Qui n'est pas tourné vers nous* (Paris: Mercure, 1972), p. 90.

[15] H. Bergson, *Matter and Memory,* trans. N. M. Paul and W. S. Palmer (New York: MacMillan, 1950), p. 195.

"in the state of invisible phantoms,"[16] that is to say forgotten in the sense of latent. The totality of the indestructible past abides there, a totality omnipresent to itself, though it is not present to my actual consciousness. "Yes, I believe," affirms Bergson, "that our past life is there, preserved down to the finest details, with nothing forgotten, and all that we have perceived, thought, and willed from the first awakening of our consciousness persisting indefinitely."[17]

Such a perennial and integral preservation raises many questions. This indestructible and inalterable past, this past always living in itself, bound to a memory "absolutely independent of matter"[18] in pure interiority, is nonetheless a past "without substance, without life."[19] Bergson's conference on the dream attributes to its adamantine memories a pretension to existence comparable to that of Leibniz's possibles, though without a clear foundation. Presented as active forces, they assert themselves in a subterranean struggle toward the "flesh" and "blood" of present sensation.[20] This "definitive" past which is kept to itself nevertheless has a horizon of futurity that seems to be properly its own, and not my project. Memories wish to accede to action, to live anew. "One must not think that memories lodged at the bottom of memory remain inert and indifferent. They are in expectation, they are almost attentive."[21] The inalterable pure memory wills a supplement, it misses the present and presence of the past that nothing in its own order can provide. The transformation of memories into autonomous substances gifted with desire and will is a construction without phenomenological foundation. But the thirst for matter that is

---

[16] H. Bergson, "Le rêve," in *Energie spirituelle* (Paris: P. U. F., 1967), p. 95.

[17] Ibid.

[18] Bergson, *Matter and Memory,* p. 232.

[19] Bergson, *Energie spirituelle,* p. 97.

[20] Ibid. Cf. pp. 95–96: when I sleep, "these suppressed memories, sensing that I have put the obstacle aside, raise the trap door that keeps them beneath the floor of consciousness, begin to stir in the night of unconsciousness. They rise up and spread around, performing there an immense, wild danse macabre," etc.

[21] Bergson, *Energie spirituelle,* p. 99.

attributed to them[22] reinforces the difficulty in other respects, since, as Bergson has said, following Ravaisson, it is matter that produces forgetting. There is no pure memory except independently of the body, it is only in the incorporeal that there could be integral preservation, and yet this incorporeality would like to incarnate. If memories wish to fill themselves and load themselves, this would be because they are empty and without weight—but then how could they be the past in its inalterable plenitude? Such is the first aporia: when everything is preserved without lack, something is nonetheless lacking. The claim that nothing is lost ends by tragically falling back into the hands *(déshérence,* "escheatment": reversion of property to the authorities) of a position it had attempted to hold off.

A second aporia pertains to the foundation of the unforgettable in forgetting. For Bergson, the "first awakening of our consciousness" is the beginning of the unforgettable, since beginning from it everything that we live is preserved indefinitely and without any loss. "Unforgettable" is not a property of certain exceptional memories, but belongs to the essence of every memory. What then of this first awakening itself? Is there a first present without past, and a first memory as preservation of a first perception? From what does this awakening awaken? Does one remember being awakened for the first time? Every inauguration has some delay, and even an initial consciousness already has a past. I was, before saying "I," and I lived some months before being born. We come to consciousness and we come to light already charged with a past. This past cannot be remembered, and could not be conserved in a pure memory. It is radically forgotten, primordially forgotten. The stated impossibility of all forgetting and loss rests on this radical forgetting, on this irreparable loss from which it secretly lives. The "original past", the "past which has never been present" that Merleau-Ponty attempts to think,[23] in solidarity with the flesh

[22] Ibid., p. 97. "Indeed, memory would like to obtain matter in order to fulfill itself, steady itself, and, in the end, actualize itself."

[23] M. Merleau-Ponty, *Phenomenology of Perception,* trans. C. Smith (New York: Routledge, 1989), p. 242.

itself, is forgotten from pure memory, from the memory that forgets nothing.

The third aporia concerns the possibility of the total presence of our past. Whether openly or secretly, the orientation of all integral conservation is an integral reactivation. This latter is, for Bergson, impossible under the conditions of incarnate life, even if, like so many others, he is preoccupied with narratives in which someone who has had a brush with death pretends "to have seen, in a very short time, all the forgotten events of life passing before him with great rapidity, with their smallest circumstance and in the same order in which they had occurred."[24] According to Bergson, this is what would happen to "a human being who would *dream* his existence instead of living it," and who would at every instant have in view "the infinite multitude of the details of his past history,"[25] but this is a matter of academic hypothesis. Bergson compares "our entire interior life" to "a single phrase begun from the first awakening of consciousness, a phrase strewn with commas, but nowhere severed by periods."[26] The inevitable question is whether one can "embrace the meaning of the phrase." Everything tends towards a total remembrance, which would be an act of total of presence of me to myself, in the unity of a meaning embraced in a single moment. In any event, it matters little whether this total remembrance is proposed as if capable of being effectively accomplished by a person in this or that state of life, or only as a teleological idea giving memory its horizon of sense. Neither of these cases can dispense with an interrogation of its meaning. This total remembrance which would give me entirely to myself and which would make me grasp myself fully, this memory of sense absolutely rendered present and presence perfectly actualized, would in truth be perfect forgetting. It would be perfect

---

[24] Bergson, *Matter and Memory*, p. 200.

[25] Ibid. One must note the insistence on the fact that not a "detail," not the "tiniest circumstance," is lost. Pure memory is, in this respect, like Amiel's private journal. [Chrétien returns to Amiel's journal on p. 58. Trans.] But is not the most profound spiritual loss signified in wanting to keep everything? Old ribbons, dried flowers, meaningless trinkets. . . .

[26] Bergson, *Energie spirituelle*, pp. 56–57.

forgetting, in reality, because it would totally abolish the past as such, as well as the relation to the past. In the transparence of a pure actuality, everything resolves itself into presence.

Thoughts of an integral conservation of the past tend toward its total parousia, which is to say toward its disappearance as past, toward itself arrival, without remainder, in presence, toward an eternal presence. Is it then the body or the spirit that puts us in forgetting? In the celebrated page from Ravaisson that features the phrase that Bergson loved to recall, there also appears in all clarity this aporia of total presence. "It is materiality," writes Ravaisson, "that puts us in forgetting; pure spirit, on the contrary, which is all action, being therefore all unity, all duration, all memory, always present to all and to itself, keeping, without ever lacking, under its regard everything that is, everything that was, perhaps even . . . everything that will be, pure spirit sees all things . . . under the form of eternity."[27] To be all memory is thus to be outside of all memory, and to be duration is to see under the form of eternity. If the relation to what I was is omnipresence to self, full possession without remainder and lacking nothing, it cancels itself out in the relation to what I *was*. When having-been resolves itself into a pure actuality, it is no longer having-been, but is as such forgotten. Plotinus was the most consequent about this when, evoking the souls of stars in the intelligible transparency of their unique act, he denied them memory. What grasps itself in a single and unique intuition without lack, loss, interval, or distance, does not have a past. To attribute one to it, says Plotinus, is as absurd as dividing a step that I take into a multiplicity of successive movements, thus transforming a single step into a multitude of steps.[28] Accordingly, to grasp myself, in a unique act of spirit, as the plenary meaning of the unique phrase that I am, is not to have conserved all of my past but to have totally lost it as the gap between me and myself.

Is it not possible that the grasp of self by self is in fact altered?

---

[27] F. Ravaisson, *La philosophie en France au XIXième siècle,* 22, ed. Millot (Paris: Fayard, 1984), p. 220.

[28] Plotinus, *Enneads* IV, 4, 7, trans. S. MacKenna (London: Penguin, 1991), p. 291.

Would I remember myself without the other? Reflecting on this, St. Augustine, too, evokes a total remembrance that tends toward an instantaneous intuition. This totally reassembled past is myself, and is no longer either past or my past as distinct from me. However, it is not my self that can do this reassembling. One must admit, says Augustine, "a kind of divine power which will ensure that all the actions, good or bad, of every individual will be recalled to mind and presented to the mind's view with miraculous speed."[29] Picking up on a phrase from *Revelations*, he compares this divine power with a book: "It ensures the recollection of the facts, and those facts are, as we may say, 'read', in this process." This is clearly to say that we are not its origin, that by ourselves we do not have the power of gathering everything completely to ourselves. The book of the inwardness of our lives, God alone can give us to read. Alterity is closer to me than is my very self. In the chapter of Leibniz's *New Essays on Human Understanding* dedicated to identity and diversity, which is where his most profound reflections on memory are to be found, he expresses some reservation at accepting such a possibility: "I doubt that man's memory will have to be raised up on the day of judgment so that he can remember everything which he had forgotten, and that the knowledge of others, and especially of that just Judge who is never deceived, will not suffice."[30] Leibniz thus admits, if only for a moment, that there were instances of forgetting concerning our own life which it would be superfluous to raise up, even at the final judgment. It seems to him neither philosophically nor theologically necessary that we deflect every review of our past into the mirror of our exalted memory. What is it that founds such a claim for superfluity?—a strong sense of the attestation of the other *(autrui)*, the word that it gives us that we have committed this or that act. Faith will pass, replaced by vision, but trust can be eternal.

[29] Augustine, *City of God* XX, xiv, trans. H. Bettenson (New York: Penguin, 1981), pp. 924–925.

[30] G. W. Leibniz, *New Essays on Human Understanding*, Book II, trans. P. Remnant and J. Bennett (Cambridge: Cambridge University Press, 1982), pp. 243–244.

A wholly other thought of memory and forgetting thus emerges here.

My past is never only mine, and is not simply kept in the secret or complete archives of my memory. What of my past escapes me, others can remember. To accept forgetting is also to accept that I am neither the only one to remember me, nor the only place where I can grasp myself. To accept forgetting is also to rely on the other for my forgetful memory, to believe his or her word about what I can neither see nor see again. The alteration of memory by forgetting does not only constitute a destruction or mutilation, but also forms the possible site of a trust. It is only through the words of others that I can know anything of the place and date of my birth, the identity of my parents and thus my own identity, as well as the validity of the name I bear. "My parents, from whom it seems that I draw my birth . . . ," says the French translation of Descartes's *Meditations on First Philosophy*.[31] Is this example of what is kept outside the reach of my memory only an exception? Can one limit the consequences? Forgetting as a loss that is always already accomplished, forgetting which founds for me the existence of the immemorial, of what leaves no trace in my memory: does this not bring out a relation to the word of the other? It can be that the others, and this is banal, help me to fill the gaps in my memory and to facilitate my attempts to remember, but it can also be, more deeply, that their memory is the place of my immemorial, for perhaps it is always the other person who is unforgettable. It will be necessary to return to these questions. But the aporiae of theories of a total conservation of the past, where everything is unforgettable, have made it necessary to briefly address them already here.

Such thoughts end in a perpetual reciprocation, a perpetual reversal of memory and forgetting into one another. Total remembrance is made into perfect forgetting, the exaltation of memory makes it disappear as relation to the past, but inversely

[31] Descartes, *Meditations on First Philosophy*, trans. J. Cottingham (Cambridge: Cambridge University Press, 1996), p. 33. Cottingham's translation reads: "From whom . . . would I derive my existence? From myself, presumably, or from my parents."

forgetting is itself the reserve of memory par excellence. This is the meaning of a famous page from *A l'ombre des jeunes filles et fleurs,* where Proust makes forgetting the truth of memory.[32] As latency, forgetting preserves the freshness of memories, and the memory entrusted to forgetting is the only memory that is unchanged—unchanged and unchangeable, because it has not been withered or weakened by habit and repetition, and because it preserves the bloom that things have at the first time. "What best reminds us of a person is precisely what we had forgotten (because it was of no importance, and we therefore left it in full possession of its strength)." The lowest of our memories, the memories we disdain, will thus be the highest and most precious, for what forgetting covers over is "the richest, that which, when all our flow of tears seems to have dried at the source, can make us weep again." Proust begins by affirming that "the best part of our memory is outside us, in a blatter of rain, in the smell of an unaired room or of the first crackling brushwood fire,"[33] and he thinks of memory as a dimension of being in the world, and of forgetting as a return of self to things and others, in trust and abandon. But this affirmation is immediately taken up and corrected. Of the reserve of the past, Proust writes: "Outside us? Within us, rather, but hidden from our eyes, in an oblivion more or less prolonged. It is thanks to this oblivion alone that we can from time to time discover the person that we were." Such forgetting thus constitutes the true memory, whereas "habitual memory" constitutes true forgetting, since from the first "the images of the past turn gradually pale, little by little, and fade out of sight until nothing remains of them." There would be nothing left of them if some words, in the example that Proust offers, had not been "carefully locked away in oblivion, just as an author deposits in the Bibliothèque nationale a copy of a book which would otherwise become unobtainable." Forgetting is the power that archives memories, conserves them, protects them, and preserves them.

---

[32] M. Proust, *Remembrance of Things Past,* trans. C. Scott Moncrief and T. Kilmartin (New York: Penguin, 1981), 1:692.

[33] See Ludwig Binswanger's remarks on this phrase, in *Grundformen und Erkenntnis menschlichen Daseins* (Zurich: Niehaus, 1973), p. 474.

It is with this view that Blanchot can write: "Forgetting is the very vigilance of memory, the guardian power thanks to which is preserved the caché of things." And on the same page, commenting on Supervielle, he has a beautiful phrase on the lunar character of memory that could also be applied to Proust: "Forgetting is the sun, memory shines by reflection, reflecting forgetting."[34]

This sort of meditation leads to the second conception of *nothing is lost*, where memory as appropriation, as the necessary condition of its meaning and function, presupposes forgetting as power of rejection. Here, forgetting is not directly that which holds and preserves, but that without which nothing could be truly preserved. Memory, if it appropriates what I acquire along the length of my own essence, if it is the very appropriation of my own essence, supposes the active elimination of what is not essential. What would we be if we could not forget? A fragment from Kafka shows us vividly: "I know how to swim, like the others, only I have more memory than them, I have not forgotten the time when I did not know how to swim. As I have not forgotten this, knowing how to swim does not serve me at all, and in spite of it I do not know how to swim."[35] The unforgettable would thus be the unsurpassable, that to which nothing can truly be added and which nothing can change. To remember the time when one did not know how to swim, to remember it perfectly, would be to once again and always reproduce this inaptitude, to once again and always fear water. As the inverse of Platonic recollection, this would be a conception of learning as forgetting—forgetting what one was, how one was, and who one was before. Were we capable of perfect appropriation of what we were, and of perfect retention of what we once were, we would be incapable of any form of apprenticeship.

To be sure, one can object to this parable that it intentionally confuses two essentially different dimensions, that of the conservation of memory and that of the maintenance of habitual

[34] M. Blanchot, *L'entretien infini* (Paris: Gallimard, 1969), p. 460.

[35] F. Kafka (in French complete works, trans. Robert, 2:586). [Chrétien cites a French translation by M. Robert, in the *Œuvres complètes* (Paris: Pleíade, 1980), 2:586. I have been unable to find this text in English. Trans.]

behavior. But is this its weakness or its strength? When memory is understood as the integration of my past to my essence, as the full presence of the past in my present being, is it not understood according to the model of habitus? The impossibility of forgetting is the impossibility of acquiring: not a gain but a loss, loss of newness and the present. In order to learn, it would be necessary to substitute the immemorial for the unforgettable, to render immemorial what we learn. What becomes totally ours becomes totally immemorial. Many theories make this the essence of memory: true memory would be to have so greatly established a power in oneself, to have made it so much one's own, that everything would take place as if there had been no beginning, as if one had always possessed it. This is the meaning of a beautiful and seemingly enigmatic phrase from Valéry: "To walk is to remember."[36] He explains it thus: "He who walks remembers how to walk—but this memory is not conscious—one does not return to the *age* of education in walking but walks as if one had always walked, and likewise [uses] words as if one has always known them." This thought is strictly parallel to that of Kafka, but presents positively what Kafka says negatively. Here, to remember is to know as if one had always known, remembering it perfectly. The possession wipes away the acquisition, and knowing forgets learning. Habitus creates a knowledge that seems to infuse us. This identification of memory with the immemorial thus makes it rest on forgetting.

This is the basis for the many panegyrics on forgetting as dissimilation that founds assimilation, or as exclusion that founds appropriation. Everything is there, always and ever, when nothing is lost except what had to be lost in order for me to truly possess, and possess myself. Never mind that one has truly and totally forgotten what it was to know how to speak, swim, or walk, if this is the condition for always knowing how to speak, walk, or swim. The *forever* of memory does not come without loss of its pre-history. No history can be unfolded without effacing its pre-history, and there is no history without lost documents. If such a conception of memory refuses and rejects

[36] Valéry, *Cahiers,* vol. 1, p. 1219.

the integral conservation of the past, this is because it is unfit to truly conserve and save. Only forgetting makes possible the exaltation of memory. Thus when Stefan Zweig, as a refugee in Brazil during the Second World War, edited his memoirs, he completed the preface by noting that he had not for all of that produced a documentary: "Of my entire past," he writes, "I have nothing more with me than what I have retained in my mind. All else at this moment is unobtainable or lost."[37] Is this lack truly a loss? "The good art of not pining over what is lost," he goes on, "has been thoroughly learned by our generation, and it is quite possible that the loss of documentation and detail may actually be an advantage for my book." For even forgetting has its laws, which make up the dignity of memory. The latter has nothing random about it, and is for Zweig the power of order and discernment. "All that one forgets of one's life, was long since predestined by an inner instinct to be forgotten. Only that which wills to preserve itself has the right to be preserved for others." The process by which forgetting loses something is thus also the process by which memory is purified and elevated. Inversely, the attempt to hold and retain everything ends in perpetual risk of intimate loss. Hence does Henri-Frédéric Amiel, wishing each night to record every hour that has elapsed, write in anxiety that "this journal is to my day what a fruit's pulp is to its flavor." The "ethereal portion" of what the soul traverses, its thoughts and feelings, "evaporate without leaving their trace." "At night," he continues, "I no longer remember them, some have vanished, others are incorporated to my spiritual make-up, and in one way or another they escape recall, and are no longer the property of my memory."[38] The calligraphy of the beautiful memory supposes an active erasure to which Amiel will not open himself, making his journal a constant escape into himself which is also an imprisonment there.

Inalterable memory, one with our very being, would be the power exercised by the art of forgetting. This is, as Nietzsche

[37] S. Zweig, *The World of Yesterday. Memoirs of a European* (Lincoln: University of Nebraska Press, 1964), pp. xii-xiii.

[38] H.-F. Amiel, *Journal intime,* vol. 1 (Lausanne: L'Age d'Homme, 1976), p. 1094.

has said, "a plastic force."[39] Every plastic force, in order to model and give form, holds up, withdraws, and eliminates. An excess of material would smother it and prohibit it. Such is the meaning of Péguy's words in *Clio:* "History is also made *against* documents. It is even made, above all, against documentary."[40] It can lack documents, but it can also, in the case of modernity, lack the lack—lack of indices, lack of references, collapsing under its own weight, perishing in overabundance. "I need a day to make the history of a second. I need a year for the history of a minute. I need a lifetime for the history of an hour . . . I need eternity for the history of the least event. I need infinity for the history of the least finitude."[41] Without forgetting, history becomes impossible. Ancient history fixes on the memorable for its object, on what is deserving of memory, of what calls for memory. Is everything memorable? Is there still anything memorable if nothing calls for forgetting? To respect is first of all to look upon something in its being, but it can also be to avert one's eyes. Shame respects. In this sense, we can and we must entrust to forgetting what asks for forgetting as the proper mode of respect. The loss of discernment between the memorable and the forgettable amounts to barbarism, for all keeping is still a manner of destroying, since undifferentiated chaos is the negation of all meaning.

The notion that forgetting is necessary for memory is the foundation of the second conception of *nothing is lost.* It is affirmed by the most diverse of thinkers, and is enough to reunite them beyond what are often very different etiologies of memory and forgetting. One must reject in order to preserve, to eliminate so that one loses nothing. Thus, Théodule Ribot, so fertile in paradoxes, arrives at the "paradoxical result that a condition of memory is forgetting. Without the total forgetting of a prodigious number of states of consciousness and a momentary forgetting of a large number, we would be unable to remember." Forgetting gives to memory its "health" and "life." "To live is to

[39] F. Nietzsche, *Untimely Meditations,* trans. R. J. Hollingdale (Cambridge: Cambridge University Press, 1983), essay 2, p. 62.

[40] Péguy, *Clio,* p. 195.

[41] Ibid., p. 193.

gain and to lose; life is constituted by the work that dissimilates as much as by that which determines. Forgetting is dissimilation."[42] Whether the etiology of memory is considered to be psychical, somatic, or psychosomatic has no decisive bearing on the questions raised here. For this fundamental analogy of an assimilating memory that rejects what it cannot makes its own and conserves something only by transforming it into itself—this vital and organic analogy traverses theories of memory that would otherwise be opposed, from the "materialist" theory of a Ribot to the "spiritualist" theory of a Louis Lavelle. The latter, for example, writes that memory is nourished on "all that appears in the world, but by means of its own disappearance, as one sees in the nourishment of the body that feeds us only in abolishing itself."[43]

This analogy is also taken up by Nietzsche in his *Genealogy of Morals.* Forgetting is "in the strictest sense [a] positive faculty of repression *(Positives Hemmungsvermögen),* that is responsible for the fact that what we experience and absorb enters our consciousness as little while we are digesting it (one might call the process 'inpsychation' *[Einverseelung]*) as does the thousandfold process involved in physical nourishment—so called 'incorporation' *(Einverleibung).*"[44] To be unable to forget is to be unable to digest, to be unable to assimilate. This does not pass, the past does not pass, and the present does not come because it remains foreign, and is not transformed into our own blood. This analogy makes of memory, properly speaking, a faculty of *incorporation* of which forgetting is one of the conditions. And this is indeed what the second of the *Untimely Meditations* describes. The plastic force of memory is what permits one to "transform and to incorporate *(einzuverleiben)* into oneself what is past and foreign, to heal the wounds, to replace what has been lost."[45] And, this passage goes on, those who do

[42] T. Ribot, *Les maladies de la mémoire* (Paris: Felix Alcan, 1883), pp. 45–46.

[43] L. Lavelle, *De l'âme humaine* (Paris: Aubier-Montaigne, 1951), p. 345.

[44] F. Nietzsche, *Genealogy of Morals,* trans. W. Kaufmann, in *On the Genealogy of Morals and Ecce Homo* (New York: Random House/Vintage, 1967), p. 57.

[45] Nietzsche, *Untimely Meditations,* p. 62.

not possess it can be bled white by the least scratch. This force makes the past into our blood, makes the past pass into our blood. "The stronger the roots that possess the innermost nature of man, the more he can appropriate himself to or submit to the past; and if one were to imagine the most powerful and prodigious nature, one would recognize that it would abolish the limit to which historical meaning could be intrusive or harmful; it would attract to itself all the past, both one's own and foreign, absorbing it and make it into blood. What such a nature does not master, it knows how to forget."[46] Forgetting re-closes the horizon of self-mastery and gives it its plenitude, as Nietzsche's subsequent analysis shows. Nothing, then, is lost of what escapes me, for forgetting serves the memory of which it is only one aspect. On this page, memory itself tends towards a whole presence, a parousia of the past. This is not repetition, reprisal, or reminiscence, which suppose a distance, gap, or tension between what is one's own and what is not, but an appropriation into the living present of blood. As assimilation, the incorporation of the past renders it present without repeating it. But is this blood where the other becomes the same, and where the past becomes present, still human blood? Is it not rather, at least virtually, on the way to becoming the *ikhôr,* the *ambroton haima,* the immortal blood which, according to Homer, flows in the veins of the gods?[47] This nature that would make all the past its own, integrate it into its blood—would it not also have all the future? Does not such a form of memory become glorious body?

It is now possible to see the proper bearing in what might otherwise appear to be a confusion between memory and habitus in Kafka's fragment on the impossibility of learning to swim when one has too much memory. The perennial possession of the past in, for, and by my very presence, the past that becomes immemorial and lives actively, circulates like blood in my pres-

[46] Ibid., pp. 62–63. On the negation of forgetting as loss, cf. the posthumous fragments of 1884–1885: "There is no forgetting in the organic domain; but rather a species of *digestion* of lived experience." *Werke,* vol. 11, ed. G. Colli and M. Montinari (Berlin: De Gruyter, 1971), p. 477.

[47] *Iliad* V, 340.

ent being, indeed supports habitus and not a representative memory. What is essential for such thoughts of memory is that *I* am unforgettable, and lack nothing. This is why I. H. Fichte, in his *Psychologie,* introduces the term "forgetting" between quotation marks. For there could not truly be forgetting if the latter would signify loss. What the mind has truly appropriated, he shows, cannot be forgotten at all, but can always be, whether willingly or unwillingly, whether by design or despite us, brought to consciousness. "Of what is truly experienced nothing is lost by the mind, even if in habitual conscious life it is there only as a latent possession. The so-called 'miracles' of memory are only expressions of its essence, or rather the essence of mind."[48] It would not be correct to say that one has "forgotten" what one has not originally taken possession of. Could one lose what was never truly ours? This permanence and indestructibility of the past, without true lack or loss, goes together with its transformation and assimilation, and, as distinct from the first conception of *nothing is lost,* supposes that memory is a plastic force. Nothing is incorporated that does not become my body and my blood, and nothing enters the mind that does not itself become mind.

Louis Lavelle formulates this thought of memory as parousia with vigor and consequence, defining it by a plenitude of time that tears free of time. To forget is to let what is lost and must be lost go to its loss in order to conquer the indestructible plenitude of our own presence. The past, says Lavelle, "is never a lost present; or at least the present that it makes us lose is only this instantaneous present which cannot be defined otherwise than by its own loss. The past is a present experience of which one can only say that we are assured of lacking it no more. We can no longer sever it from our own life: it is at once immutable and available."[49] From there, it is said that our memory satisfies a triple function with respect to the given: "interiorizing, whereas it [the given] is present to us first of all as coming from

[48] I. H. Fichte, *Psychologie* (Leipzig: Brockhaus, 1864), § 193, pp. 413–414.

[49] L. Lavelle, *De l'âme humaine,* p. 346. The next citation is found on the same page.

outside; spiritualizing, whereas it always affects a material form; and immortalizing, whereas it belongs to becoming and does not cease to die away." Memory "thus as it were absorbs time into eternity."[50] Memory would then be the place where we free ourselves from time; it transcends the past, and abolishes the relation to the past as such in order to reach the timeless presence of essence. This parousia where the whole past is illuminated and dissolved into indestructible presence, where every exterior becomes interior, and where all suffering and submission reverses into act, evaporates time into the quiet blaze of eternity. When nothing is lost everything is consumed, the first memory already testifies to the end of time, and the theory of memory becomes eschatological. Even Schopenhauer, who sets little store by memory and never mentions it except to show its weakness and imperfection,[51] nonetheless sees in it a manifestation of our functional timelessness: "The very freshness and vivacity of memories from the most distant time, from our earliest infancy, are proof of the existence in us of a principle which does not follow time in its revolutions, but which, without aging, subsists sheltered from change."[52] This is the case *a fortiori* when the parousia of our past can be complete. Thoughts of the conservation of the past are oriented to the possibility of regaining it in a unique act of transparency and life: it is of little matter whether this act really is, according to these conceptions, that of a glorious body of a transfigured spirit. When Proust suggests that the resurrection of the body after death may be conceivable as a phenomenon of memory,[53] he expresses in reverse order a rule of all thoughts of *nothing is lost*: memory tends toward a resurrection or a parousia. To speak of it is to speak of an apocalypse, even if it can be depicted quite diversely. But if this were to be so, then what would it mean to forget forgetting? Of what would that forgetting be the forgetting? Why this life without

---

[50] Ibid., p. 358.

[51] A. Schopenhauer, *The World as Will and Idea,* trans. R. B. Haldane and J. Kemp (London: Kegan Paul, no date), 2:334–335. Cf. *Über die vierfache Wurzel des Satzen vom zureichen Grunde,* § 45.

[52] Schopenhauer, *World as Will and Idea,* 3:387.

[53] Proust, *Remembrance of Things Past,* 2:786f.

loss or lack? Does it tend toward a future parousia, or is it not already at bottom parousia, where I am my own savior, which is to say an idol?

The stake of this forgetting of forgetting, this negation of loss in its very possibility, is the negation of death. The parousia of memory does not traverse it and does not break through it, but ignores it. In gathering what passes into the unchanging, the least memory is, in these theories, already the proof of immortality. This is why they display a fundamental opposition not between forgetting and memory but between forgetting something of the world and forgetting oneself. Forgetting has nothing serious about it, above all if it is only the other face of memory, when I can never forget myself or miss myself. It matters little what I lose, if this loss is never loss of myself, nor of this blood that always comes to enrich.

Does it suffice, in response to all of this, to deny this parousia, to affirm an insurmountable forgetting, and to pose, in principle, the excess of the past over my memory, in order to then recognize what the thoughts of *nothing is lost* live to forget? In his phenomenological study of *Vergegenwärtigung und Bild*, representation and image, Eugen Fink asks if it is possible that the totality of the past of the transcendental ego is disclosed by acts of memory. "Is it possible that every 'point' of the past is, as it were, convertible by remembrance?"[54] He answers strongly in the negative. No subject of understanding—and Fink says this even of God, understood as limit concept—can grasp through memory the totality of its past. In receding ever further, the chain of memories "interrupts itself and loses itself in impenetrable obscurity," and this "obscurity preceding all possible remembering" has nothing either accidental or contingent about it, but possesses an essential necessity. "The world is thus *always already* constituted," and the transcendental ego that constitutes it and renders it possible as world could not through memory render it contemporary with its first constitution. The

[54] E. Fink, *Vergegenwärtigung und Bild.* (The Hague: Nijhoff, 1966), § 16. [Chrétien cites a French translation by D. Franck, *De la phénoménologie,* (Paris: Minuit, 1974), p. 52. Trans.]

retrospection of genesis could not reach transparency. There is thus, to borrow an expression from Husserl's studies on passive synthesis, a "night of forgetting" (*Nacht der Vergessenheit*), and on this night there could never come a day that totally lights it up, dissipating the darkness.[55] In other words, the "phrase" to which Bergson compared our life [p. 51] does not have a beginning, but is always already underway. With this, phenomenology has discovered a forgetting that does not reduce to a provisional and rightfully surmountable latency: here there is no parousia of the past.

Yet, what the impossibility of this parousia reveals is an *always already,* an "unconsciousness that is nothing less than a phenomenological nothingness, yet a limit-mode of consciousness."[56] This undefined horizon of the past that memory can never fully revive, regain and render present leads in the final account to the grasp of its proper eternity. "Transcendental life and the transcendental I can not be born, it is only man in the world who can be born. I, as transcendental I, I am eternally (*Ich war ewig*); I am now, and this now belongs to a horizon of the past that can be unfolded to infinity. And that itself means: I was eternally."[57] To this past without end corresponds a future without end. Forgetting of self is only an obfuscation, a condition of my presence. This obfuscation is positive, sheltering my eternity. There again, forgetting forms the reserve of memory, an inexhaustible reserve, attestation of what does not begin and has not begun, and which will also never end.

Can one ever untie this bond that makes every praise of forgetting a praise of memory, and transforms loss itself into a proof of parousia? It seems, in a wholly other space of thought, that Plotinus escapes this difficulty. When he affirms that the good soul is forgetful, this is not a matter of conditional forgetting, of a forgetting in the service of memory, but of a veritable

[55] E. Husserl, *Analysen zur passiven Synthesis,* ed. Fleischer, Husserliana, vol. 11 (The Hague: Nijhoff, 1966), Beilage 8, p. 377.

[56] E. Husserl, *Formal and Transcendental Logic,* trans. D. Cairns (The Hague: Nijhoff, 1969), p. 412.

[57] Husserl, *Analysen zur passiven Synthesen,* p. 379. Cf. p. 378: "The nothing before the beginning already presupposes something."

effacement and a veritable loss of what made our earthly life. When at his death Hercules returns to the intelligible world, can he and must he retain a memory of those works and exploits which for us make up the very meaning of his name? Or must he instead show a vigor and a force greater than he himself had exhibited in those works, but now for the struggles fought by the sages?[58] These are the struggles of forgetting. What will it cost to make the act of having swallowed or strangled monsters intelligible? Plotinus eliminates any memory of the presence of the soul to the purely intelligible. Once purely in the intelligible, the soul cannot have "any memory of experience here. There can be no memory in the intelligible world, not merely none of earthly things, but none whatever."[59] This abandon of memory as abandon of everything with which memory is in solidarity goes all the way to forgetting of self. The philosopher himself, in attaining what he sought for his entire earthly life, forgets even having searched: he does not remember that he was here a philosopher. And should he contemplate really being one "there will not even be memory of the personality; no thought that one who contemplates is the self—Socrates, for example."[60] All during his contemplation, he no longer knows who he is, nor what he is, soul or mind. It does not seem possible to bring the affirmation of forgetting, and of a definitive forgetting, any further. There is indeed parousia in this, but a parousia that is not of memory, does not render the past present, and does not let it efface itself totally in place of regaining it. Faust's phrase that "the trace of my earthly days can not disappear across eternities"[61]is the exact contrary of what, according to Plotinus, can be and must be the case. Eternal light must dissolve every trace, understood as every trace of the path followed in order to reach it.

What is the meaning of this forgetting of our temporal life?

[58] Plotinus, *Enneads* IV, 3, 32, p. 285.

[59] Plotinus, *Enneads* IV, 4, 1, p. 286.

[60] Plotinus, *Enneads* IV, 4, 2, p. 287. [MacKenna's translation reads "intellectual" where this text reads "intelligible." Trans.]

[61] Goethe, *Second Faust,* Act V: *Es kann die Spur von meinen Erdetagen/ Nicht in Äonen untergehn.*

To be sure, it is loss, but what does it lose? It does not involve loss of this or that memory, but the disappearance of memory itself, as a faculty. This forgetting is perfect amnesia, elevation above the region of being where the weight of memory holds us. In the purely present contemplation of intelligible eternity, every memory would cast a shadow. To contemplate in such a way that one is united with what one contemplates, is to forget and to forget oneself, to lose oneself in light. For Plotinus, I become this light where I lose myself, and my highest truth is to be found in its plenitude. There where each of us is his or her own site,[62] how could there be the tension, the distension of memory, according to which I am here and elsewhere, according to which I am at my own having been? The intervals of memory are abolished into coincidence. In this light, I do not lose myself in order to *re*discover myself, in which case the path could never be wiped away, but in order to at least truly find myself, in order to coincide with the pure essence of intelligible self that I have never ceased to be. To know that one is Socrates is to know oneself as man, not as spirit. But to know oneself as man is to cease to be everything, as indeed I am in the intelligible.[63] Knowledge of self as spirit is, for Plotinus, beyond memory, understood as memory of self, because it is beyond all return to self. I know myself in knowing everything, which is to say in becoming everything, and not in reflecting on myself. There again, everything leads toward a parousia of the eternal, and forgetting forms only the loss of the loss, or in other words what other thinkers call by the name of memory. Once again, nothing is lost of what escapes me, even if a radical forgetting is affirmed.

From there, however, there may still be posed some questions that go beyond the limits of Plotinus's thinking. The fact that memory unveils and forgetting veils, that the former discovers and the latter covers again, even if to shelter it, and that forgetting is latency, obscurity, obfuscation—such is the common sun under which the foregoing theories are to be found.

---

[62] Plotinus, *Enneads* V, 8, 4, pp. 414–415. Cf. VI, 7, 13, pp. 482–484.
[63] Plotinus, *Enneads* V, 8, 7, pp. 417–418.

With Plotinus there appears a possible light of forgetting, and a possible obfuscation by memory. How to get out of the circle where forgetting keeps hold of something and where memory keeps watch over it—how to escape the *nothing is lost?* Is the future of the past necessarily omnipresence to self, whether it is conceived as that of pure spirit gathering itself into a faultless "yes", or as that of a glorious body somehow incorporating everything? To what is that "yes" said? Is it only the return that it makes us expect, and for that reason forget nothing?

To retain or reject, to conserve or not conserve: such alternatives cannot suffice for a meditation on memory and forgetting. To the form of memory that St. Thomas Aquinas calls sensitive—bound necessarily to corporeal being, and incapable of being the fact of pure spirit or a separated soul—belongs a relation to the past as such, *praeteritum ut praeteritum.*[64] It is only through incarnation that we turn toward the absent in so far as absent, that we are beings of the distance *(du lointain).* Only a being of slowness and heaviness can be in the distance and of the distance, for it is from the interval this marks, from the most intimate moment of itself, that it knows patience and pain. In a beautiful page in the great Chinese novel *Si Yeou Ki, Journey to the West,* some genies able to cross immense distances in a single bound must concede their powerlessness to transport a single man. Their master is of earthly flesh, and therefore, for them, heavier than Mount T'ai Chan. They do possess power to shrink the earth, to shorten distances, and move mountains. But their master must accept the conditions of corporeal beings; it is only by one step at a time that he can go from one place to another.[65] This weight that no magic can take away is that of the incarnate spirit. It is also this alone that makes it possible for us to remember and forget. We can no more be magically transported in time than we can in space. Hence the correctness of what a character from Faulkner's *Wild Palms* finally grasps: "But memory. Surely memory exists independent of the flesh.

[64] Aquinas, *Summa Theologiae,* Ia, q. 79, art. 6.

[65] Wou Tch'eng Ngen, *Si Yeou Ki. Journey to the West,* trans. W. F. J. Jenner (New York: Foreign Language Press, 1993), chapter 22.

But this was wrong, too. Because it wouldn't know it was, *he thought.* It wouldn't know what it was it remembered. So there's got to be the old meat, the old frail, ineradicable meat for memory to titillate."[66] Without the flesh, we could not learn what this is by heart, *par cœur,* according to the beautiful French expression. Incarnate being is by itself power of recalling and remembering, not because the past is inscribed of itself in it in the form of material traces, which are always only present and of the present, but because it alone opens us and relates us to what we can remember. If there is memory only of the past, incarnation is the condition and the place of all memory.[67] When Ludwig Binswanger renders our power to recall something forgotten, and to bring to consciousness what was unconscious, consistent with our flesh—when he thus makes it the very place of memory—it is only to fall back immediately into questionable views. For he adds that "we could not forget something if we do not exist in corporeality. A being thought to be without anything corporeal—God—can not forget!"[68] This is to withdraw all force from the thought of the body previously expressed, in favor of restoring an incorporeal body as the paradigm of a pure memory without forgetting. God does not forget in the sense that we forget, but God also does not remember in the sense that we remember. Even concerning a finite being, the acts of an intellective memory that repeats its intellections and conserves its habitus do not constitute memories.

The relation to the past as past, in solidarity with the flesh, is not the negation of loss, as if the act of recalling the past would suppress it as past, then revive it, and render it once again and fully present. Rather, the relation to the past as past is what renders the loss present. One remembers only what is lost, lost forever, never returning. To turn by memory toward the past as

---

[66] W. Faulkner, *Wild Palms* (New York: Modern Library, 1984), p. 316, cf. p. 324.

[67] This does not rule out that the term *memory* could be given a much larger sense, as occurs in Augustinian thought. But it seems better to preserve the image that binds *memory* to the past, even if one also admits a memory of the present or the eternal.

[68] L. Binswanger, *Ausgewälte Vorträge und Aufsätze,* vol. 1 (Berne: Francke, 1947), p. 155.

such is neither to repeat it nor to make it come back, but to aim at it and await it in its very distance. When we are absorbed and lose ourselves in the past through the reveries that occult the present acts of remembrance by which we recall it, there occurs a remembering that forgets itself as memory. Husserl has described this admirably.[69] This dreamy loss of self, this immersion where the present ego and its presence are as if placed in a sleep that abolishes the distance as such, and makes me become in some fashion *ichlos*, without ego. Even if this past where we forget ourselves can have its own allure and its own fascination, nourished precisely by our forgetting, it is without the glory so frequently named by the poets: the glory of the past, of an absolute past, is discovered only by those who do not forget themselves as the subject of remembering. This glory shines according to the loss. It is the glory of what is lost, of what is, as Baudelaire has said, "already farther than India or China."[70] The distance that is intimate and temporal is expressed as a distance that is exotic and spatial. It is expressed with as much force as there is in a question ("is it already farther . . . ?") and a movement of distancing that does not permit one to assign it a specific distance. Wordsworth's ode, "Intimations of Mortality from Recollections of Early Childhood,"[71] shows this vividly, making the absolute distance of a pre-existence[72] emerge by beginning from the absolute distance of memories of childhood and their unique glory. The word *glory*, invested with a meaning close to the theological meaning, is repeated often throughout the ode. But the poet sees it as glory only in its disappearance:

The things which I have seen I now can see no more

---

[69] Husserl speaks of *Selbstvergessenes Erinnern*, in *Analysen zur passiven Synthesis*, pp. 306–309.

[70] C. Baudelaire, *Flowers of Evil*, ed. and trans. J. McGowan (Oxford: Oxford University Press, 1999), LXI, *Moesta et errabunda*. Merleau-Ponty also cites this verse, in his reflections on the architectonic past evoked below (see p. 72, this volume).

[71] W. Wordsworth, *Wordsworth. Representative Poems*, ed. A. Beatty (New York: Doubleday, 1965), pp. 662–669.

[72] See the fifth strophe: "Our birth is but a sleep and a forgetting," and the poet's explanation in prose (pp. 661–662), referring to "the notion of preexistence as having sufficient foundation in humanity" to authorize poetic use of it.

And:

Whither is fled the visionary gleam?
Where is it now, the glory and the dream?

The inner distance and its abyssal growth, the impossibility of gathering oneself together, of filling the gaps that form in ourselves, remembrance makes us discover with a singular clarity. From there comes the ever resilient and ever desperate character of the enterprises of a total parousia of the past, where we would be our own memorial. Baudelaire reminds us of the importance of this when, in the same passage cited above, he asks of the paradise of childlike lovers:

Can one restore it with plaintive cries,
And bring it back to life with silvery tongue?

The single voice, and not the gaze, could restore it to presence, but could never overcome its own alteration, could not itself become once again the silvery tongue of childhood.

Fear of forgetting is not fear of losing what we possess, but fear of losing what is already lost. For loss of the loss does not form a double negation that would amount to an affirmation. In order to suffer loss, it must be that what is lost tends toward disappearance and distance, where it is manifest in what was unique and irreplaceable about it. The loss that holds again and retains what it has lost can lose itself, letting the distance distance itself without accompanying it with its own tearing *(déchirement*—both ripping and heart-breaking). In his *Vie de Rancé*, Chateaubriand writes of the sacrifice that he, Rancé, has made of letters and portraits: "To break with real things, this is nothing; but with memories! The heart is torn at separation from dreams; there are few such realities in man."[73] To sacrifice memories taken in this sense, and all the dreams that weigh on them, that deny or disclaim loss, is certainly not to lose memory. It is, on the contrary, to confide them solely to our memory, and not to episodes, to replace them with a memory without a

[73] F.-R. Chateaubriand, *Vie de Rancé*, in *Œuvres romanesques et voyages*, vol. 1, (Paris: Pléiade, 1969), p. 1051.

handbook, conserving them as completely lost, and in this pure memory exposing them to forgetting. But is it truly from dreams that Rancé separates himself in making letters burn? Do we also appeal to *memories* of things of the world? Does the pain of this separation show the power of the imaginary, as Chateaubriand says, or does it rather show its powerlessness? Is it not born of knowing that there is in the color and grain of paper, in the curl of script, the fading of ink, more than there is in any image, and that without seeing them I could remember only having forgotten them? Should we not hear in this a confession of the carnal character of memory?

Only this irremediable distance and this halo of loss give to our memories their essentiality and their character of absolute past. The will to recover oneself through them in a parousia is thus bound immediately for failure. Merleau-Ponty evokes what he calls the "architectonic past" that "belongs to a mythical time, to time before time, to the anterior life," even if this anterior life is a matter of our infancy.[74] Such a past is certainly foundational, but it founds by collapsing, founds by the radicality of its loss and disappearance, becoming timeless and immemorial. This timeless past is raised in us from all time, not as what is absolutely outside time, but as what is absolutely past and thus essential. As soon as these dimensions are taken in view, there appear exchanges between memory and forgetting other than those that have been discussed until now. The desire to retain everything and never lack anything oneself is already, in the end, exposure and, as it were, openness to the forgetting that it refuses. It struggles against this excess of the past over memory, and it denies it, but would not do so without having recognized and in a sense confessed its reality. Those who do not wish to lose anything at all are already lost, according to a perdition that they could not lift.

In *Either/Or,* Kierkegaard opposes aesthetic and ethical existence, and shows that the former, though it remembers all sorts

[74] M. Merleau-Ponty, *The Visible and the Invisible,* ed. C. Lefort and trans. A. Lingis (Evanston: Northwestern University Press, 1968), p. 243. [Text of "Working Note" dated April 1960; Lingis translates "prior life." Trans.]

of things, does not have the memory of its own life, whereas the latter remembers itself, though it will have forgotten much.[75] Why so? Ethical existence, as opposed to aesthetic existence, lives according to the decision, which is to say according to the promise. Only a promise can bind the sheaf of memories as well as accept that many are lost. Bergson's notion of an alignment of memories one after the other, without loss or lack, is totally unreal. Only the promise, which alone can unify my life and make a history, is capable of gathering them. But it does so only in preserving the memory of its future, only in remembering what it has promised and the power from which it has promised it; it thus gathers them only elsewhere and far away. There is nothing irreversible except through the promise. Access to the unforgettable, far from being retention and conservation of indestructible memories, passes through loss and through forgetting. This is why, speaking of the instant "when a person links himself to an eternal power for an eternity, where he accepts himself as the one whose remembrance time will never erase," where one becomes unforgettable—Kierkegaard can write: "It is as if you lost yourself, as if you ceased to exist."[76] This unique instant where one binds oneself forever is only a birth because it is also a death. It permits me to find myself only by not rediscovering myself. It founds memory of self, but without denying forgetting. What is lost in it is truly lost—which is why it gives.

Every promise has its witness, and none is witness for itself. Every promise has someone to whom it is destined, and none is destined for itself. Its end is also its origin: it receives itself and I receive myself through it, in giving itself and order to be given, but it must receive the capacity to be given. And from whom, if not from the other (*l'autre*)? We begin, and truly begin, only in promising, but we never begin already at the promise. If there is a parousia, I am not it and I cannot be its place. Its place is exodus. For the excess of the past over my memory is not only my own lack of myself, and not only the impossibility of fully

[75] S. Kierkegaard, *Either/Or. Part II*, in *Collected Writings*, vol. 4, trans. H. Hong and E. Hong (Princeton: Princeton University Press, 1987), pp. 197 and 230–231.

[76] Ibid., p. 206.

coinciding with me. It is also and first the excess of the encounter over my own possibilities. For there are no other memories than those of our encounters with people, living beings, and things, thus with what was excessive in the very present of the event, in the very present that shatters us, that prevents us from rejoining ourselves and satisfying ourselves, and in the best case makes us forget ourselves.[77] Could one recollect without having received, and without having given? To have given is also to have received, for those to whom we give give us first of all their giving. The only excess of the gift is the light of the unforgettable. It never comes without promise. To be able to incorporate, as certain theories would like, my past—my entire past—would amount to incorporating everything. It would amount to becoming one with the world. Can one consider recollection in this way? Or should we think of it as my own incorporation, through memory and through forgetting, to a body of which I am only a member? How could there be in me and by me a perfect coalescence of my memories, when all these memories are ecstatic and always remember only what gets lost, forgotten, given? If our memories are in reality outside of us, as Proust said before correcting himself [p. 55], it is that they are never anything but memories of encounter. In them, more was given to for me to experience than I could experience, more than what I could expect and receive—and this "more", which is all that is truly important here, is what memory forgets when it wishes to retain everything, determine everything, store everything away, and incorporate everything.

The excess of the promise over my possibilities, which makes it anything but expectation or foresight, responds to the excess of the past over my memory. Our memories are not only bounded by forgetting as if by a horizon, and they do not only emerge on the ground of forgetting as from an obscure back-

[77] On the power of the encounter, see the page where Binswanger evokes a melancholic who goes into a forest with the intention of hanging himself, and at the very instant when he is about to do so, is torn away from death by the striking contemplation of. . . . a weasel, an animal he had never seen before that moment. In L. Binswanger, *Melancholie und Manie* (Pfullingen: Neske, 1960), pp. 55f.

ground; forgetting crosses them and inhabits them like the mark of what slips away from them, of that in which they render their inspiration *(souffle)* and give it. Forgetting prohibits not only a parousia of the past, but also a full presence in the present itself. To respond from myself is in reality to respond from more than I could see, see again, and know, and the place where I could respond is not my own presence regained and recapitulated, but is there where my promise is entrusted and given elsewhere, in the other. Kierkegaard thus writes in his *Gospel of Suffering,* concerning the pardon that brings forth a new life: the past is not purely and simply forgotten, "but is forgotten in the pardon. Each time that you remember the pardon the past is forgotten, but when you forget the pardon, the past is thus no longer forgotten, and the pardon is lost."[78] It is not a matter here of an interlacing of memory and forgetting comparable to thinkers discussed earlier. For this forgetting does not come under a power of our forgetting, and it has an importance wholly opposed to the forgetting that we could produce ourselves, as by a consequence of our memory. This is shown well on the same page, in terms of an opposition between the "melancholic spirit," who wants nothing to be forgotten, which causes the pardon to be forgotten, and the "free spirit" who wants everything to be forgotten, including the pardon. Both put to work a power, or a powerlessness, which belongs properly to us. The other forgetting of which Kierkegaard speaks is the light borne by the pardon in so far as we make it our own, which is to say in so far as we receive it. To this received gift, it is the "yes". Only the unforeseen excess of a new life permits the overcoming of the past, concerning which Schelling observed so forcefully that without it we do not have a past.[79] This forgetting does not wipe away my faults, as if it were only an amnesty expunging my criminal record. It is rather of a single piece with the remit-

[78] S. Kierkegaard, *Upbuilding Discourses in Various Spirits,* in *Collected Writings,* vol. 15, trans. H. Hong and E. Hong (Princeton: Princeton University Press, 1993), p. 247. [Translation adapted to Chrétien's terminology. Trans.] Cf. the analysis by G. Gusdorf, *Mémoire et personne* (Paris: P. U. F., 1950), 2:368–369.

[79] F. W. J. Schelling, *Werke,* ed. M. Schröter (Munich: Beck, 1959), 4:635.

tance of my faults not only *by* the other, but also *to* the other, who alone can respond to them entirely. To remember the pardon is to remember, in the present, the one who gives it. Memory of God, this remembering is the source of every promise that we can make.

The mystical theology of John of the Cross shows powerfully the bond of forgetting and hope understood in the highest sense. He writes in *The Dark Night:* "Hope empties and withdraws the memory from all creature possessions, for as Paul says, hope is for that which is not possessed. It withdraws the memory from what can be possessed, and fixes it in that for which it hopes. Hence, only hope in God prepares the memory perfectly for union."[80] The emptiness and destitution of memory—deprived, truly deprived of its treasures, and where, after all, every treasure first arrives—are not its destruction but its purification, its elevation, and its transfiguration enacted by God. In order to fulfill itself, and in order to receive God himself in hope, memory must pass through forgetting, must enter into forgetting. Forgetting is the incandescent point of memory, that which comes in contact with the inferno. In *The Ascent of Mount Carmel,* John of the Cross says again: "The memory must be rid of all notices and forms (i.e., sensible things), and lose its perception of them . . . in such a manner that there remains no notice impressed in it, nor any trace of anything, smooth and bare, as if it were not in the world at all."[81] Memory, wholly sovereign as it is, would be "in great forgetfulness, without the remembrance of anything" (*en grande olvido, sin acuerdo de nada*[82]). This emptiness and this night of memory, accomplished in the "great forgetfulness," raise it up toward He who alone can fulfill it; they withdraw it from all the substitutes that could never satisfy its hunger and its thirst. We will not be

[80] John of the Cross, *The Dark Night of the Soul,* II, 21, 11, in *Collected Works of John of the Cross,* trans. K. Kavanaugh and O. Rodriguez (Washington, D.C.: Institute of Carmelite Studies, 1979), p. 381. On these questions, cf. A. Bord, *Mémoire et espérance chez Jean de la Croix* (Paris, 1971).

[81] John of the Cross, *The Ascent of Mount Carmel,* III, 2, 3, in *Collected Works,* p. 215.

[82] Ibid. Cf. the text in *Vida y Obras de Juan de la Cruz,* ed. L. Ruano et al. (Madrid: Biblioteca de Autores Cristianos, 1973), p. 561.

saved by dried flowers. Forgetting, the great forgetting, is the offering to God of memory, because God inhabits it. It will be recovered after this night, but in different form; it will have become malleable, receptive to divine action, instead of being the organ of attachment to what escapes it or has already escaped. Because memory is the place of presence, it must be stripped of its memories and lose them, putting out its candles under a greater and, indeed, properly excessive light. Forgetting alone, if it is great, places us in accord with this excess. For this will not be of our presence. The emptying of memory constitutes a sort of death and heartbreaking, painful, loss. It purifies us of our adhesion to this inner treasure where the world rushes ceaselessly. The emptiness of memory is "a yearning and a melting away of the soul for the possession of God," says John of the Cross in another place, before citing the lamentations of Jeremiah.[83]

There is something exceptional in this supernatural filament of memory. It nevertheless manifests what the night of forgetting can make of it, in destining it and ordering it to its end, becoming the memory of the Other. Wounded by the forgetting that dispossesses it, it is in love that it is wounded. We are not unforgettable. Only the immemorial is properly unforgettable, when it is given in hope and gives hope, by and in forgetting. Coming without returning, it comes without return, outside every repetition, making all things new. And with it, it bears the memory of what it gave us to give, of what we have lost without trace or remainder, that which has immediately escaped memory, for we never knew what passed through us. As we bear it, it does not give itself again, but gives itself as the very excess of its presence that no memory can contain. All the rest, which we strive to hold and retain in our inability or unwillingness to give it, is always already bound for forgetting, for it is always already dead.

[83] John of the Cross, *The Living Flame of Love,* Commentary, 21, *Collected Works,* p. 618.

3

The Unforgettable

WHAT IS IT that cannot be forgotten? How are we to think what would forever escape from the forgetting, what withdraws from all forgetting and all hiding? From the moment when, over against theories which contend that everything is forgettable and nothing is either lost or darkened, the power of forgetting is indeed recognized, we must ask whether it is nonetheless possible to immediately contain that forgetting by assigning it an unsurpassable limit. If one grants that true forgetting is possible, one cannot suppose that the unforgettable would only be its simply formal, exterior, or contingent characteristic; the unforgettable could not simply define the indeterminate force of my memory as faculty, faultlessly but also arbitrarily conserving whatever memory it chooses, but would have to be something that belongs properly to what does not lend itself to forgetting—to what, in itself and, as it were, in advance has a luminosity that nothing can extinguish or conceal. The unforgettable would not designate the pure permanence of a memory put perpetually at our disposal, but would found this very permanence and make it possible—that is, supposing that it does take place.

The idea that the past as such could be unforgettable in precisely this sense is one that commands our attention. How and to what degree could the past escape forgetting in principle, if not also in so far as it could never become merely the past, in so far as it would not pass and would not be passed by? This is why the Greek word *alastos*, which in the most direct sense means "unforgettable," is applied almost exclusively to trial, mourning, and suffering, and defines them in their essence. In Ancient Greek speech, it is not our joys that are unforgettable, but our trials, those experiences that hollow out in us, and in spite of us, the space of the unbearable. "Unforgettable" is a suffering from which we have no power whatsoever to withdraw. It may even be better to say that it is it that does not forget us. The "unforgettable" thus does not designate a property that is conferred by memory and that manifests the vigor of memory, but the very pains that strike to prohibit and disarm our capacity for forgetting. In this sense, the word does not properly refer to a memory. Hence does Hesiod say, in the *Theogony,* that "a sorrow beyond forgetting" gripped Rheia[1]—she whose children Kronos swallowed, one by one, as they were born, out of fear that one among them would dethrone him. This unforgettable pain renews itself without cease, and does not send the goddess to its past but marks the living site of an affliction. And what afflicts is the interruption of the future, immediately taken back up into a present that persists and will always persist. In Aeschylus's *The Persians,* emperor Xerxes, distressed by the cries of the chorus enumerating his vanished warriors, exclaims: "In truth, you do recall me to my yearning for my gallant comrades, when you speak of woe surpassing woe, hateful and unforgettable. My heart within me cries aloud for those hapless ones."[2] Without doubt, this is an expression of remembering and recall *(hypomimneìskeis),* but the exposure to the unforgettable *(alasta),* appearing in the neutral plural, far from being an *Erinnerung* by which memory takes up and preserves in itself, interiorizes, certain events, is what makes the heart cry out, what tears it from itself in its silent interiority toward the world where Xerxes's companions no longer are. The unforgettable is presence of absence, poignant permanence of the unbearable. In Sophocles's *Oedipus at Colonus,* finally, the word *alasta* is uttered by Oedipus to describe trials that are in fact indescribable. When the chorus begins to say, "You have suffered . . . ," Oedipus cuts them short, saying, "I suffered woes unforgettable."[3] The fact that he has suffered this shows that he does not

---

[1] *"Rhéèn d'ekhe penthos alasthon," Theogony* 467, in *Hesiod,* trans. R. Lattimore (Ann Arbor: University of Michigan Press, 1959), p. 150.

[2] Aeschylus, *The Persians* 987f, in *Aeschylus,* trans. W. H. Smyth (New York: Putnam's/Loeb, 1927), p. 193.

[3] Sophocles, *Oedipus at Colonus* 538: *"Epathes/Epathon alast' ekhein."* Trans. H. Lloyd-Jones, *Sophocles* (Cambridge: Harvard University Press/Loeb, 1994), p. 475.

cease to suffer it, and not that he remembers it without ceasing. Unforgettable suffering is in the present; it does not concern memory in any way. Suffering has a passive ecstasis, an aspect that does not cease to throw us outside of ourselves, rendering us incapable of finding refuge anywhere, even in ourselves. Unforgettable is this vis-à-vis from which there is no shelter whatsoever.

This is why, according to a well-known paradox,[4] the first gift, and all the more so the highest, of Memory par excellence, of the mother of the Muses, Mnemosyne, is the gift of forgetting. Which forgetting would this be, if not that of the unforgettable such as it has just been defined here? Of the Muses, Hesiod says: "Mnemosyne, queen of the Eleutherian hills, bore them in Pieria, when she had lain with the Kronian Father; they bring forgetfulness of sorrows, and rest from anxieties."[5] *Mnèmosunè, lèsmosunèn:* the assonance and affinity of the name of Memory and that of forgetting are underlined by their presence at the beginning of these two verses. Memory engenders the gift of forgetting, forgetting of misfortunes, a forgetting that we could neither produce nor attain ourselves. And far from coming from silence, this forgetting is in solidarity with speech, song, music, the guardian powers of the senses. To the ecstasis of suffering is opposed the ecstasis of the word. It is not in us or by us that we can forget; hence is it the case that what there might be to forget is not in us but in the world. In order to forget, one's heart must be abducted by the world, discovered in its joy through song, since it is also in the world that one does not cease to suffer. In the course of the *Theogony,* Hesiod returns to this forgetting: "When a man has sorrow fresh in the trouble of his spirit and is struck to wonder over the grief in his heart, the singer, the servant of the Muses singing the glories of ancient men, and of the blessed gods who have their homes on Olympus, makes him presently forget his cares, he no longer remembers sorrow, for the gifts of the goddesses soon turn his

[4] Cf. M. Detienne, *Les maîtres de vérité dans la Grèce archaïque* (Paris: P. U. F., 1973), pp. 69f; M. Simondon, *La mémoire et l'oubli dans la pensée grecque jusqu'à la fin du Vième s.* (Paris: Les belles lettres, 1982), pp. 128f.

[5] Hesiod, *Theogony* 53–54, trans. R. Lattimore, p. 126.

thoughts elsewhere."[6] To the burning, destructive light of new misfortune which, since it is unforgettable, would always be new, to the suffering which one cannot be rid of, song opposes the power of distance: it calls to the distance and in the distance, the distance of time and that of space, of the heroic and divine condition, the distance of height *(hauteur)*. It enchants and delights in height, and it consoles precisely because it does not seek to console, because it does not ease mourning and does not argue with sorrow, but tears us from the insurmountable presence of our pain and misfortune by another presence, a presence that is distant. The patience of consolation cannot make one forget: it can only make one support the insupportable. By enveloping us in the glorious light of heroes and gods, whose poetic speech constitutes in itself the proper and indispensable space of brilliance and permanence, song makes one forget the unforgettable in the only way this can come about—*quickly*. The final two propositions in fact begin with an adverb of time signifying rapidity.[7] This promptness of forgetting that is opened by speech has no distraction or diversion in it. It is true that it turns us away from suffering, but this detour is toward what remains, toward what is properly and in itself memorable.

It is thus in the other and through the other that we forget and that we remember. Speech comes from a divine Memory that never becomes ours, even if it does dispense its favors and gifts on us in offering another unforgettable, that of our misfortunes. Yet neither of them is a secret kept jealously within us. It appears here and now that the unforgettable is bought with the price of forgetfulness. This price is not comprised of the selection and assimilation of memories, as is found in the thoughts of *nothing is lost* studied in the previous chapter. The unforgettable is a light where another light is extinguished, a light whose excessive radiance makes the light of our candles disappear and be lost, but without this being a matter of wiping out traces, imprints, or residue.

---

[6] *Theogony* 98–103, pp. 128–129.
[7] *Aipsa* (102) and *takheôs* (103).

Aristotle displays a vision wholly other than that of Hesiod, when at two points in the *Nicomachean Ethics* he reflects on what would not be lost through forgetfulness. But for him, too, it is not a matter of a memory withdrawn in advance from all forgetfulness, according to some enigmatic privilege, and the unforgettable does not essentially concern our relationship to the past. For Aristotle, it is inadmissible to suppose that there is anything in us that cannot fall into forgetfulness and obsolescence. Among the aptitudes, capacities, and faculties that we have acquired, some are more stable and more durable than others, and less exposed to a possible forgetting. The unforgettable has an axiological sense: the degrees of the unforgettable are the degrees of excellence and perfection of an activity. And this is not an accidental qualification, coming from the exterior—coming, for example, from memory—and adding itself to such an aptitude: rather, it is determined by the very nature of the aptitude. This is why what is highest in ourselves and of ourselves is nothing other than unforgettable. Thus, in the first book of the *Nicomachean Ethics,* Aristotle asks whether happiness comes to us from good fortune or from our own activity—evidently a question consistent with that of its duration and stability. In order to differentiate science from opinion, Plato had insisted on the stability of the former, which, once attained, could not easily be lost. For Aristotle, still more stable than scientific knowledge are virtuous activities. "And at among these virtuous activities themselves," he writes, "the most deserving of honor are also the most lasting, because those who are happy pass their lives exercising them in preference over all the others, and because they can exercise them in a more continuous fashion than they could all the others: this has every appearance of making the argument that in the matter of virtue there is no forgetfulness."[8] The object of science is the necessary and the permanent, but we are not able to exercise our scientific knowledge at every instant. And one would thus cease to do it in a lasting way, since the absence of exercise makes us lose that knowledge, just as exercising it made us acquire more of it. As

[8] Aristotle, *Nicomachean Ethics* I, 11, 1100b14–17.

opposed to this, St. Thomas says, commenting on Aristotle's text, "we are constantly presented with occasions in which it is necessary to act according to virtue, or against virtue, such as during the consumption of food, when in the company of women, in conversations with men, and all things of this sort, with which human life never ceases to be involved."[9]

It is therefore impossible to forget virtue by ceasing to exercise it for want of occasion to act according to it or against it. Since this occasion presents itself at every instant, in pressing manner, and whether we wish it or not, virtue could not fall into obsolescence such as can happen when one forgets an art or science that one no longer practices. Concerning prudence, or wisdom *(phronèsis),* the sixth book of the *Ethics* reprises the same thought. The fact that wisdom is a virtue and not an art, that it does not reduce to a "habitual state which would only be reasoned," shows that it cannot "disappear due to forgetfulness," as can indeed happen with art and science.[10] Morality is unforgettable, since we always desire happiness, and because no inadvertence, no break from habit can take place in this order. The unjust person could not be exonerated by alleging to have forgotten to be just. The latency of the good cannot coincide with that of forgetfulness, but is bound only with a recovery from injustice through choices and positive acts. Not having practiced justice in a long time amounts to having been for a long time in injustice, in as much as the occasion for justice and injustice is never lacking and in as much as we must choose at every instant. In the two uses that Aristotle makes of it, the argument for what can and cannot be forgotten serves as a criterion for discerning the nature and conditions of the exercise of a human activity. The act that qualifies as unforgettable would be any act that is the most continuous possible and for which there is unceasing occasion to exercise it. The unforgettable does not concern my origin, but my end. It reduces neither to remembering nor to the past, for, as the object of ethics, it puts

[9] Aquinas, *In decem libros ethicorum Aristotelis ad Nicomachum expositio* (Turin: Marietti, 1964), §§ 188–190.

[10] *Nicomachean Ethics* VI, 5, 1140b28–30. Cf. Aquinas, op. cit., § 1174.

into play what I must do and what I must be. It is by its very nature that it does not permit being forgotten. In losing it, I would not diminish my memory, but miss my ultimate end. It is bound partly with the future.

The thought of the unforgettable is thus not one of an impassable remembering to which memory ceaselessly adheres and which it would ceaselessly represent. It is not the object of memory, the result of its operation, or the mark of its vigilance, but is what gives memory to itself, the gift whose favor makes memory possible. In *What is Thinking?*, Heidegger meditates on the original meaning of the German word *Gedank,* thought, and hears in it the word *Gedächtnis,* memory. But the latter is not at all reducible to the "faculty of mental representation of something that is past." Rather, its essence lies in "the gathering of thought upon what everywhere demands to be thought about first of all. Memory is the gathering of recollection, thinking back. It safely keeps . . . everything that essentially is, everything that appeals to us as what has being and has been in being." Even the act of retention, as the defining act of memory, "is attached not only to the past, but also the present and the future."[11] This perspective on memory in all of its amplitude, according to which it is also memory of the present and of the future, belongs to the Augustinian tradition. Only this can remain faithful to a sense of the unforgettable that does not make it the retracing of an extenuating memory of the present, and by the same stroke render it increasingly empty.

Thus, in his *Itinerarium Mentis ad Deum,* St. Bonaventure does define memory by *retentio, retinere,* but states that the past is only one among its possible objects. "The operation of the memory is retention and representation, not only of things present, corporeal and temporal, but also of past and future things, simple eternal. For memory retains the past by recalling it, the present by perceiving it, and the future by foreseeing it."[12] Retention is thus articulated in several acts which are es-

---

[11] M. Heidegger, *What Calls for Thinking?,* trans. F. D. Wieck and J. Glenn Gray, in *Basic Writings*, D. F. Krell (San Francisco: Harper and Row, 1977), p. 352. [Translation modified. Trans.]

[12] Bonaventure, *Itinerarium Mentis ad Deum* III, 2.

sentially distinct, as are their objects. And as the "heart" would later be for Pascal, so the memory, according to St. Bonaventure, is the certain knowledge of principles of the sciences and of quantities—e.g., point, instant, unity. It is with these principles in mind that he writes memory "can never forget them" *(nunquam potest sic oblivisci eorum),* for it does not cease to "recognize [them] as being innate and familiar to it." These evident truths do not reduce to the content of a memory. They are rather its condition. Were we to forget them, then nothing more would be perceived, grasped, and retained as what it is. Only the unforgettable at the heart of memory makes possible all its operations. It is always already there; its first cognition *(connaissance)* is always for us a re-cognition *(reconnaissance)* and an assent. Thus understood, the unforgettable is what gives the mind thinking, that without which it would not be mind. It is this that gives importance to the medieval play on words relating mind to memory, *mens dicatur quod meminit*, "one calls mind that which remembers."[13] Before all remembrance in the current sense of the word, before all representation of a past event, our memory already remembers the unforgettable. Its opening to the unforgettable is not a movement that it would accomplish in a single constitutive instance, it is not reducible to the initiative of memory, but is precisely what initiates it and founds it.

In the history of thought, it is rare for the unforgettable to be thematized at length, and moreover the word does not seem to be a fundamental term for philosophy. But each time that it is named, even fugitively and, as it were, by detour in a phrase, it makes up the decisive moment. All thought has its unforgettable, and it is in naming it that a thought recognizes that to which it is dedicated and destined, as well as its own promise—which does not mean that such a thought always keeps its promises. Thus, when Malebranche evokes the "ineffaceable idea of being," he writes this admirable phrase: "One can indeed some-

---

[13] Guillaume de Saint-Thierry, *De natura et dignitate amoris*, § 33. [Many of the writings of Guillaume are available only in Latin and French—which, moreover, Chrétien frequently modifies (see below, note 20). English translation is therefore directly from his French. Trans.]

times be without thinking of oneself, but it seems to me that one could not subsist a single moment without thinking of being."[14] The mind breathes only through being, which is more original to us than ourselves. We are of being more than of ourselves. This unforgettable and incessant presence of being to mind is not an object for the mind, but the mind's very opening, its only light, and its condition of possibility. Having taken memory in a narrower sense than it has in the medieval tradition, Malebranche does not consider it the place of the presence of being. But there is still something of the unforgettable in this. Whatever its proper designation, it is what does not cease to come in having always already come, and it is that whose incessant coming is the condition of all appearance. In that same sense, it could not come to face us, to be embraced and comprehended by the mind. But how are we to think its relation to the future?

In his *Buch der Freunden,* the poet Hugo von Hofmannsthal recalls a remark from Goethe that shows the future of the unforgettable, as well as the fact that without the unforgettable no future could take place: "He who does not remember the good, does not hope."[15] The incessant coming of the unforgettable to memory conserves nothing of the congealed, ossified past, but shines from the very brilliance of the future. It is not a matter of repeating what we would have experienced, nor a matter of either returning to it or making it come back. When in the *Philebus* Plato shows that there is no desire without memory[16]—for one could not desire what is absolutely unknown to us, and what would satisfy the desire is precisely what we lack and is not there—he does so with the example of hunger and thirst, understood as an emptiness that one must fill. Memory reminds us of past satisfactions and thus permits us to desire; it is the principle of repetition.[17] When there is hope, such a repetition is not in

[14] Malebranche, *Recherche de la vérité,* III, 2, 8, 1; in *Œuvres complètes,* vol. 1, (Paris: Pléiade, 1972) pp. 456–457.

[15] H. von Hofmannsthal, *Buch der Freunden* (Frankfurt: Suhrkamp, 1985), p. 59: *"Wer sich des Guten nicht erinnert, hofft nicht."*

[16] *Philebus* 35.

[17] The aporia of the first desire and first fulfillment has not escaped the Platonists.

play, and one must therefore think another relation between memory and desire, a future (*avenir,* a coming-to) which is not a return (*revenir,* a coming-back).

As the memorial of our end, memory does not remember it as a beatitude once known or possessed. St. Augustine's thought brings this out vividly. *Memoria Dei,* the memory by which we relate ourselves to God, is not at all a remembrance. The paradise lost is totally lost; it is the object of faith and not of reminiscence. To tend toward beatitude is not to wish to reclaim Eden or any anterior state of humanity. Of man, Augustine writes in his treatise on the Trinity, "certainly he does not remember his happiness. That was once, and is no more, and the mind has totally forgotten it and therefore cannot even be reminded of it. But he believes" by reason of the Scriptures alone.[18] Nostalgia for Eden is not a Christian thought, for Scripture cannot be replaced by remembering. There is no way back, not even in thinking. On the same page, Augustine, evoking the memory by which the soul remembers God, again tears it away from any past: "Not that it remembers him because it knew him in Adam, or anywhere else before the life of this body, or when it was first made in order to be inserted into this body. It does not remember any of these things at all; whichever of these may be the case, it has been erased by oblivion." This forgetting has nothing provisional or surmountable about it: the necessity of Scripture here comes precisely from the fact that it is the only possible memorial of what is radically inaccessible to our memory. Something is forever lacking in the treasury of memory, and St. Augustine, who elsewhere has shown how lapses of memory are only consignment to latency and not destruction, here gives full right to forgetting as loss. The unforgettable does not live from a negation or from a denegation of the loss.

Adhering to an Augustinian perspective in studying the images of the Trinity in the human soul, Guillaume de Saint-Thierry says that God placed the power of memory at the summit of the soul "so that it would always remember the power

[18] Augustine, *The Trinity* XIV, xiv, 21, trans. E. Hill, O.P. (Brooklyn: New City Press, 1991), p. 387.

and the goodness of the Creator." Memory of the eternal gives us the continuity of time, according to our sense of the *always*. As the image in us of the Father, the memory engenders reason, and the memory and reason both engender will. Guillaume goes on: "In truth, the memory possesses and contains the aim toward which it must tend *(memoria habet et continet quo tendendum sit);* reason comprehends that it must tend; will tends."[19] The memory of our ultimate end does not seek repetition. Memory destines us; it is the place of the promise because it remembers that which promises. It alone opens the future forever. What is essential in the work of Guillaume de Saint-Thierry is this bond between memory and desire. Memory possesses only the pledge and the glimmer of what is promised to us. And it possesses only in being itself possessed and carried off. The *Expositio super Cantica Canticorum* says it forcefully: "His memory was already filled and entirely possessed by a crucifying will, or a desire, that is to say a vehement will."[20] And the *Enigma fidei* formulates the sense of this movement in unmistakable terms. The unforgettable presence of God to memory forms one of the elements of the image of God in us. This image can be covered over or deformed by evil, but it could never be destroyed. This is because it is inadmissible that we might tend toward its reform and accomplishment through grace. "That I always remember you, that I think of you, that I love you, until, faithfully remembering you, thinking of you with prudence, really loving you, O Trinity who are God, according to the plenitude that you know, you reform me in your image, according to which you have created me."[21] The ceaseless coming of God to memory, by which he is unforgettable, does not signify that we hold the absolute within ourselves, nor does it imply that we could enjoy it in withdrawing into an interior

---

[19] Guillaume de Saint-Thierry, *De natura et dignitate amoris,* § 5.

[20] Guillaume de Saint-Thierry, *Commentaire sur le Cantique des cantiques,* § 76. We have frequently modified the French translations without signaling it on each. On memory in the thought of this great mystical theologian, cf. Y. A. Baudelet, *L'expérience spirituelle selon Guillaume de Saint-Thierry* (Paris: Beauchesne, 1985), pp. 46–49. [Chrétien's modifications have been followed in the English translation. Trans.]

[21] Guillaume de Saint-Thierry, *Enigme fidei,* § 26.

fortress. God comes to memory in order to strike it with a wound of love that eternity itself could not close again. And this influx that tears us open shows that he has set his heart on us in creating us in his image.

This image of the eternal has a history. And it is only in being the image of the eternal that it does properly have a history. The unforgettable does not state a plenary and non-temporal presence. It is present only as call and appeal, in its very coming. This annunciation of God to memory does not at all signify that we do not have to seek God, to desire God, and to tend towards God, for it is only if God manifests himself to us, precedes us, and foresees us that a desire for him is possible. He alone has and can have the initiative. To call God unforgettable is to say that we are forever, at the most inward part of ourselves, transpierced by his light, and not that we would always suffer it in the same way. What could a person attempt to cover up and veil, if not such a light? What could one attempt to flee, if not such an encounter? What could one try to fill in by any means, if not such a fault? And what could one desire to forget, if not the unforgettable? It is what can neither be totally lost nor totally abandoned, in our flight and in our refusal. Of the soul, St. Augustine says: "Yet it is reminded to turn to the Lord as though to the light by which it went on being touched in some fashion even when it turned away from him."[22] It is not enough to close our eyes, to initiate the reign of darkness.

From the very fact that one might seek to forget the unforgettable, it follows that one also has to remember it. The unforgettable is in no way something that would dispense us from fidelity or render fidelity superfluous. It is what properly requires fidelity and, requiring it, renders it possible. In truth, one can have to always remember only what by its very being calls for such a remembrance, and requires this constancy and fidelity. To have to ceaselessly present the mind with such empirical detail would be to lose the mind, and not to accomplish it or vivify it. What calls incessantly to memory must itself be manifest as incessant, having given something of its plenitude in order to be able to

---

22 Augustine, *The Trinity* XIV, xiv, 21, p. 387.

promise it as our end. The vow to always keep in memory does not create the unforgettable; it is what responds to it. It responds through the future of what does not cease to come. The unceasing calls for a fidelity that is always new, and it alone can require this. The unforgettable is not adequate to our memory, but immediately exceeds it, and in exceeding it destines it.

How are we to think that this unforgettable is excessive? Is it not by definition that to which I am always present, that which I always regard without possibility of even losing it from view? Is there not in this a perfect appropriation into central presence? Is not what surpasses my capacities for vision and grasp therefore what escapes me, thus what I forget? It is thanks to the thought of St. Augustine that it is possible to approach the unforgettable presence of God to memory in its singularity: "But you, you were more inward than my most inward part and higher than the highest element within me" *(interior intimo meo et superior summo meo).*[23] Far from being a central object, God is eminently radiant for our memory, for what makes us present to ourselves;[24] God is present to us only in comprehending us and exceeding us on every side. His presence is eschatological in the strict sense of the word, a presence at the extremes and to the extreme, a presence that is immediately given only in excess and in surplus *(interior, superior).* The unforgettable is not what we perpetually grasp and what cannot withdraw from memory, but what does not cease to grasp us and from which we cannot withdraw. The fact that it is indissociable from our being in the image of God shows that what gives us our ownness remains inaccessible and beyond appropriation. For the image, in so far as image of the infinite, always manifests the excessive, which we must love and respect, but which is not at all at our disposal.

Yet this unforgettable demands some forgetting as the price for manifesting the fidelity that we bear it, for there is no aban-

---

[23] Augustine, *Confessions* III, vi, 11; trans. H. Chadwick (Oxford: Oxford University Press, 1991), p. 43.

[24] Cf. the definition of memory in *The Trinity* XIV, xi, 14, p. 382: "the faculty by which the soul is present to itself" *(qua sibi praesto est).* [Translation modified. Trans.]

don to excess without loss and sacrifice. If memory of God must be Christian, it could not escape death and resurrection. And this can be to extremes without calling for some extremity from our side. Such is the meaning of the expression by St. John of the Cross: *Olvido de lo criado, memoria del Criador,* forgetfulness of the created, memory of the Creator.[25] The forgetfulness of the created can in no way produce or stimulate the memory of the Creator, for this would be to put created and Creator on the same plane and suppose commensurability between them. Not even the forgetting of the finite can make memory of the infinite emerge. It is therefore necessary that what is primary is this memory by which God himself comes to our mind. But our fidelity to this gift lies in willing to receive still more, in tending toward what it promises, and in paying the price of the forgetfulness that responds—and can only respond—to the unforgettable.

In the Epistle to the Philippians, where among other things the very expression of kenosis is established, St. Paul writes: "I press on to make it my own because Christ Jesus has made it his own. No, brothers, I do not consider that I have made it my own; but one thing I do, forgetting what lies behind *(ta men opisô epilanthanomenos)* and straining forward to what lies ahead, I press on toward the goal for the prize of the upward call of God in Jesus Christ."[26] Existence by faith is bound indissociably with memory and forgetfulness, in so far as it is of hope. Forgetfulness itself is gift; it belongs to the fidelity of the response. Having been grasped by God precedes and exceeds all our grasping: we respond to this anteriority by forgetting it. This forgetting does not reduce to the forgetfulness of the old man, or to the forgetting of sins in the remembrance of the pardon. It takes part in the movement toward that which renders all things new, and which does not cease to render them new. Even what in me has already been rendered new must be forgotten, for I myself am not the site where I must contemplate it. Re-

[25] *Vida y obras de San Juan de la Cruz,* ed. L. Ruano et al. (Madrid: Biblioteca de Autores Cristianos, 1973), p. 416.

[26] Philippians 3:12–14. [All bible translation from the Revised Standard Version, with occasional modifications. Trans.]

garding the newness in me would end by rendering it caduke, and would give me the illusion of being able to grasp it, whereas it is it that grasps me. I must go the course with what in me has been rendered new. Commenting on this phrase from St. Paul, Guillaume de Saint-Thierry gives meaning to the paradoxical expression "perfect travelers." How can a traveler be perfect? Perfection as accomplishment and as achievement, by which a being is brought to its final end, seems to exclude every course or way. "They are perfect in that they forget what is behind them and turn toward what is ahead of them; they are travelers in that they are still on the way."[27] There is thus, for Guillaume, a perfection of forgetting as such. It is the human response to the unforgettable. For what is ahead is nothing other than the unforgettable promise of Christ Redeemer.

Forgetting inscribes in memory the very excess of the *memoria Dei* over the *memoria sui.* The former can never be contained by the latter. This is why the importance of forgetting, in this tradition, is not at all the same as that of forgetting in the thoughts of *nothing is lost* studied in the previous chapter. To be sure, in the one case as in the other, forgetting serves memory and permits it to fulfill itself. But the meaning of this supporting role for memory changes radically according to whether it is a matter of freeing myself and bearing the memory of my proper life to its greatest plenitude, of redeeming it and relieving it of everything non-essential and everything superfluous, purifying it of what I cannot make my own forever and completely, or rather of forgetting myself in what is mine and in what I have already made mine, in order to remember the Other and his promise. St. Paul truly renounces a return to himself and a grasp of himself: through forgetting, loss, and sacrifice he enters into faithfulness to having been seized by God. Faith is essentially remembrance, but remembrance of God's promises, and it thus constitutes the place where remembrance is transfigured into hope, passing through the fire of forgetting—a fire which burns and consumes every memory of our own in us. To such a transfiguration, this fire would be the obstacle and

[27] Guillaume de Saint-Thierry, *Enigma fidei,* § 23.

screen *(écran)*. He who wants to save his life will lose it, and memory also makes up a part of this life that we would like to save at any price. In order to hope in remembering, and to remember in hoping, which makes up faith, one must lose something of one's own memory. When we remember an event from sacred history, such as the Nativity, this memory hopes, because it also calls and awaits the Christ born in our hearts. But he can be born only in a heart as poor as a manger, a heart that is empty and dispossessed, and this memory thus also asks for forgetting, forgetting of self as offering.

How far does this forgetting go? In the completely hymnal page that he dedicates to the dereliction of Christ, Jules Lequier, in an audacious formulation, attributes a singular forgetting to Him. In this prayer, the recognition of Jesus as God takes place *sub contraria specie*, through the very cry of dereliction: *My God, my God, why have you forsaken me?* And Lequier reflects that "He who was the light suppressed by darkness, the wisdom who no longer knew! The swallowing up of the redeemer into the depths of an abyss of suffering where, in the ecstasis of pain, he lost even the memory of what he had come to seek there, yet without losing his treasure."[28] This wisdom which Jesus' human consciousness no longer knew, no longer knew as wisdom, does not enter reflection, yet for all of that does not cease to be. It is accomplished as such in this very non-knowing, which once and for all takes up into itself and assumes body and soul all ignorance, all darkness, all incomprehension where we were, are, and will be in pain, fault, and evil. It no longer knows because it is given. This is why pain is an "ecstasis," a being outside of oneself, and not a closure into oneself. The "treasure" that Jesus does not lose is not he who was, but he who is; it coincides with his mission and with his being sent. And the forgetting that Lequier attributes to him is one with the very accomplishment of this mission, since the following phrase evokes "this unique Son, eager for brothers who won. . . . in the horror of this formidable abandon," taking upon himself all the sin of the world, and from the very inner-

[28] J. Lequier, *Œuvres complètes* (Neuchâtel: La Baconnière, 1952), p. 450.

most depth of his throat let forth this nocturnal and yet luminous cry—nocturnal, since he cries out in abandon at the darkest moment of history, and yet luminous, since he assumes it with all the force of God. And it is this that redeems all human abandon, understood as the experience of thinking oneself abandoned by God. Such a forgetting signals the unforgettable as the night signals day, fraternally, for Psalm 22, which Jesus cites in this cry,[29] ends in praise and speaks of a time when "all the ends of the earth shall remember and turn to the Lord."[30] This forgetting in Jesus' human consciousness, of "what he had come to seek," is not all a privation or an eclipse: it is the moment of coincidence and unity between the gift and the giver, for the sacrifice of self, if it is perfect, leaves neither time nor space to even think of this sacrifice. The fire burns without having to remember to burn, and by this it is a pure fire and its burn unforgettable. Whether or not one assents to Lequier's formulations of the mystery of the dereliction (and they are in the purest tradition of the French school[31]), it remains true that what the Christian faith commemorates in the existence of Jesus—and without possibility of forgetting this—is that he does not cease to be forgetful of self, even in the perfect gift and most complete sacrifice. It is there alone that *memoria sui* is not exceeded by *memoria Dei,* and forgetfulness of self thus shines in it as the unforgettable gift.

This excess of the memory that we have of God over the memory that we have of ourselves plays a capital role in the

[29] In what sense can one speak thus of citation? Do we really know what a citation is? This unique word from the unique Son is in any case what one calls a citation, just like those words that he pronounces outside of temptation. In order to state his own dereliction, he does not invent words that are his own, but restates what has indeed been said in prayer before him. But for Christian faith, this disappropriation of the word of abandon is also a radical appropriation, at least if one interprets the Psalms *in persona Christi.* It is indeed his words that one repeats.

[30] Psalm 22:27. In the biblical weave of memory and hope, future memory is here the very object of hope.

[31] Cf., among many other texts, F. Bourgoing, *Méditations sur les vérités et excellences de Jésus-Christ Notre Seigneur recueillies de ses mystères, cachées en ses états et grandeurs, prêchées par lui sur la terre et communiquées à ses saints,* meditation XIX, vol. 2 (Paris: no publisher given, 1892), pp. 439f.

Augustinian thought of the image of God in us. Studying the faculties of the soul, St. Augustine discovers there an image of the divine Trinity, in as much as the soul "remembers itself *(meminit sui)*, comprehends itself, and loves itself." But, properly speaking, "it is his image insofar as it is capable of him *(ejus capax)* and can participate in him."[32] The subsequent chapter of *De Trinitate* affirms this clearly: if thus the trinity of the soul is the image of God, "this is because it is able to remember and understand and love him by whom it was made."[33] These words provide the full meaning of what is said in the *Confessions*: what is most inward in the mind is the power to turn toward something still more inward than itself, and what is highest in it is the power to turn toward something that transcends it. The alterity of God is inscribed unforgettably at the heart of our inwardness. And this memory of God that founds our very being is nonetheless essentially inadequate to what it remembers without coinciding with it. It can remember it neither fully nor totally, and it can make it become present only as it is present to itself. This memory is not the place of the parousia. It is the very excess of the unforgettable that is rigorously manifest in our memory.

For St. Augustine, the *memoria Dei,* unforgettable and inexhaustible presence of alterity, is necessarily at work in all the spiritual exercises that we might possibly commit, but it does not reduce to a determinate practice and does not designate a specific spirituality. It is wholly otherwise with the *mnémé theou* that plays an important role in the monastic tradition, and above all its Greek current.[34] There, it is a matter precisely of living in incessant memory of God, and in such a fashion that he penetrates into all our acts and thoughts. In his treatise on the contemplative life, Philo of Alexandria already uses the expression,

---

[32] Augustine, *The Trinity* XIV, 11, p. 279.

[33] Augustine, *The Trinity* XIV, 15, p. 383. "Understand" translates *intelligere,* and is evidently not a matter of an "understanding," in the strict sense, of the divine essence.

[34] The historical and theological study of this expression would be rich and complex, but is unnecessary here. Cf. G. Lange, *Bild und Wort* (Würzburg: Schöningh, 1968), Exkurs II, *Bilder eis anamnesin und die Spiritualität der mneme Theou,* pp. 182–200.

concerning Therapeutes: "Always and with forgetting *(alèston)*, they preserve the memory of God *(tèn tou théou mnèmèn)*, so that even in their dreams they see nothing but the beauty of the divine excellences and powers."[35] It is in this way that the thoughts of perpetual prayer are engaged. But there again, the unforgettable requires an exercise of forgetting, for the ancient tradition sees memory as one of the places par excellence for temptation and distraction to the praying monk. There is no meaningful ascesis that would not also be ascesis of memory. "Intelligence," says Evagrius Ponticus, "has a terrible tendency to let itself be overturned by memory during time of prayer."[36] With memories, the world penetrates completely into the monk's cell, forcing him into sadness, disgust, melancholy, and nostalgia. In this connection, Fr. Hausherr cites a text where it is said that demons seize and plunge the soul "into the sadness of what things no longer are and can no longer be, being given the form of present life." To the memory of God as site of hope is opposed the memory of ourselves as site of regret. To what end would one withdraw from the world, if one would continue to be there, in an impassioned and disordered manner, through memory? What memory can be completely serene? The unforgettable must therefore always be undergone and watched over: it is not the durability of a memory engraved once and for all on our memory. It breathes only through its future, which is always new, and it characterizes a life that is thrown and projected, beyond its own possibilities, toward what God has promised it.

To watch over the unforgettable would, by its ever excessive nature, form a desperate undertaking were we to be its initiators solely by our own works and efforts. To be sure, we do watch over the unforgettable in a manner that is indispensable and absolutely proper to us. For we can always wish to forget the unforgettable, and fidelity always has, in its very peace, something violent and agonistic about it. It is to the promise that we are faithful, but we must promise to be faithful to it, and to not

[35] Philo of Alexandria, *De vita contemplativa*, 26. *Philo of Alexandria*, vol. 9, trans. F. H. Colson (Cambridge: Harvard/Loeb, 1941), p. 127.

[36] I. Hausherr, *Les leçons d'un contemplatif, Le traité de l'oraison d'Evagre le Pontique* (Paris: Beauchesne, 1960), § 44, pp. 67f. Cf. pp. 23f.

forget it. The exiled of Psalm 137 can and must say: "If I forget you, O Jerusalem, let my right hand wither! Let my tongue cleave to the roof of my mouth, if I do not remember you."[37] As pledge of their fidelity, they offer their hand and their voice, those things that make one human. To forget Jerusalem would be to longer be oneself. But it always remains possible, as a question simply of one's very self, to lose one's voice and hand. To no longer be oneself is an essential possibility of the self. We ceaselessly forget that what we have said can never be forgotten. The unforgettable to which we are faithful would be a place of fear and trembling if we were its only authors and witnesses.

Its origin and end are held in the promise of him whose memory we must watch over. God will not forget us. The fact that he does not forget cannot be thought exclusively in metaphysical terms. Undoubtedly, being pure spirit, God does not have any limitations or weaknesses from which something like forgetting is possible. However, aside from the fact that this argument supposes a uniquely privative thought of forgetting, the God that it evokes could be thought wholly other than as the Savior. In an eminent sense, God forgets, forgets the offenses. To say that not being finite he can forget nothing, thus by nature, is to affirm only the negation of the negation. If God does not forget us, it is because he is the God of the promise, the faithful God. We are not unforgettable for ourselves and by ourselves, and to seek this for ourselves be would be to render ourselves idolatrous; it would be to conduct ourselves into pure loss. But we are unforgettable for God, for his faithfulness is unwavering. He affirms this himself in the book of Isaiah: "Zion said, 'The Lord has abandoned me, my Lord has forgotten me. Can a woman forget her suckling child, that she should have no compassion on the son of her womb? Even these may forget, yet I will not forget you *(Et si illa oblita fuerit, ego tamen non obliviscar tui)*.'"[38] Human faithfulness par excellence signals toward divine faithfulness. But it does not furnish the ultimate measure of divine faithfulness. Even if the improbable were to

---

[37] Psalm 137:5–6.

[38] Isaiah 49:14–16.

occur—if a mother were to forget her child—still, God would not forget it. And even if we forget Jerusalem, and our hand withers, the hands of God eternally bear the unforgettable. The following verse says: "Behold, I have graven you on the palm of my hands." Who could wipe away what God has graven on his hands? The hands of the glorious body of Christ bear forever their scars *(stigmates)* of the unforgettable, as an eternal memorial of time and history. The unforgettable that we watch for and watch over is founded in an unforgettable for God and by God himself. Its source is found in the unhoped for.

4

The Sudden and the Unhoped for

THE EXCESS of the event over the look of expectation can show simply the finitude and fallibility of human understanding. But it can also be understood positively as the mark of an origin that is more than human. Frequently, the radically unforeseen and completely unhoped for character of what happens appears as the signature of divine power at work. Every divine action disturbs: it foils our expectations and our calculations, our hopes and our fears, in a striking manner. Such a shock, showing that we are not the measure of the divine, and that the divine escapes us at the same moment that we do not escape it, relates us to it essentially. The unexpected does not have only a negative sense when it reveals a power and an aim other than our own. In the event that cuts us short and puts right every illusion of mastery, the divine is not solely what escapes our comprehension, but also what advances toward us, seizing us and acting on us in that very escape. This approach to the unexpected brings up the ancient theme of the ambiguity of the oracles. Even when the gods proclaim what they will do, announce to us their plans, we do not expect what will finally takes place, for we interpret their words in the horizon of our own expectations and our own desires. The mistakes of Cresus in the first book of Herodotus's *Histories*, illustrate this well. And even when the gods grant our petitions and give us what we ask, they can do it in such a way that what we obtain is in reality wholly other, and produces consequences that are wholly other than we had imagined. Seeing one's desire fulfilled can be as terrible and as surprising as seeing it disappointed.

There would be no tragedy without this flaw of the unexpected, where the human and the divine are separated and meet. Superabundance of meaning is heavier to bear than lack of meaning. Euripides says this forcefully when he completes several of his tragedies with the following verse: "There are many shapes of divinity and many things the gods accomplished in a manner unhoped for. What one looks for is not brought to pass, but a god finds a way to achieve the unexpected. Such was the outcome of this story."[1] How must we understand this "unexpected," this *aelptôs*? Is it even best to translate this word as "unhoped for" *(inespéré),* or only as "unexpected" *(inattendu)*? Has Greek religion known a hope against all hope? *Alcestis*, which ends with this verse, seems to manifest such a hope. Thanks to the favor of Apollo, Admetus is spared from having to die on the appointed day. But in order for this to come to pass someone had to voluntarily undergo that death in his place, and give tribute to the Fates. Everyone gets out of this sacrifice until it is his wife Alcestis who is substituted for him, and Euripides's tragedy is situated in the day in which she must die. Right away, the space proper to this piece is constituted by a tension and a weave between the necessary and the unhoped for. That it is possible for someone to not die at his or her appointed time, thwarting the punctuality of Thanatos, is the unhoped for. And this unhoped for has a properly divine origin, coming from, as the prologue insists, Apollo's intervention. But the unhoped for, if for an instant it tears the tissue of necessity and opens some light there, could not actually destroy it, and it is necessary, without any possible evasion, for Alcestis to die that death, at the time which would have had to been her husband's but has become her own. Admetus, the untamed—for such is the meaning of his name in Greek—has been able to slip outside the reaches of Thanatos, but Thanatos remains as untamed as him, and cannot not come to take Alcestis, his substitute victim.

The greater portion of this tragedy lies in the shadow of this

[1] Euripides, *Alcestis* 1159–1163, trans. D. Kovacs, in *Euripides* (Boston: Harvard University Press/Loeb, 1994), p. 281. [Translation slightly modified in accordance with Chrétien's text. Trans.] The other tragedies ending with this verse are: *Helen* (1688f.), *Bacchae* (1388f.), *Medea* (1415f.), and *Andromaches* (1284f.). Cf. V. Goldschmidt, *Temps physique et temps tragique chez Aristote* (Paris: P. U. F., 1982), pp. 405f.

immanence of an ineluctable death. The unhoped for goes together with the without hope, in the exchange of destinies. "There is no cure for evil."[2] "Is there no hope that her life may be saved? No: her fatal day presses on."[3] To be sure, before Alcestis's death, just as after it, the chorus sings prayers that hope for the unhoped for—that Alcestis, in her turn, will also escape. "Her fate is plain, my friends, all too plain, but still let us pray to the gods: the gods' power is supreme."[4] But these prayers, according to their impossible wish, quickly become the expression of mourning more than of hope. "Would that it lay in my power and I could escort you to the light from the halls of Hades by an oar plied on the nether stream of Cocytus!"[5] In this same chant, the only true immortality recognized of Admetus's wife is that which she will receive, in the words of the poet, words which will not cease to proclaim her love and her sacrifice.[6] And as a result, those words will appear as if weightless on Necessity, *Anagkè*. "Of that goddess alone there are no altars, no statue to approach, and to sacrifice she pays no heed." Even he who has "lived with the Muses" in the end finds only this: "Nothing is stronger than Necessity, nor is there any cure for it in the Thracian tablets set down by the voice of Orpheus," poet par excellence, nor the remedies of Apollo. It has tamed Admetus the untamed.[7] The same unhoped for that has been accorded him has become the occasion for despair, and the added life won for him by the sacrifice of his wife no longer presents him with either joy or meaning. And were one to stop here, the story of Alcestis would indeed be the tragedy of the unexpected, but not of the unhoped for.

At the end of the piece, however, Heracles, who has been hosted by Admetus, restores Alcestis to him, carrying her from Hades and the subterranean deities. She who was lost, lost forever, is regained, and Alcestis is granted more joy than Orpheus.

[2] *Alcestis* 135, p. 173.
[3] *Alcestis* 146–147, p. 175.
[4] *Alcestis* 218–220, p. 181.
[5] *Alcestis* 455–459, p. 205.
[6] Cf. *Alcestis* 445–459, pp. 445–454.
[7] *Alcestis* respectively 972f., p. 259; 962f., pp. 258–259; 982f., p. 258.

This is indeed a matter of the unhoped for in the strongest sense, for it is no longer susceptible to reversal into its contrary. Seeing the living Alcestis, and having difficulty believing his eyes, Admetus pronounces the word: "O gods! What shall I say? Here is a miracle unhoped for *(thaum'anelpiston tode).* Is this truly my wife I see here?" he exclaims, before addressing her: "O face and form of the wife I love, I have you back in a manner unhoped for *(aelptôs).*"[8] The adverb is the same as in the conclusion of *Alcestis*, and is completely unequivocal. Were one to possess only this one among Euripides's tragedies, one would still have to interpret the aforementioned conclusion on divine action as a hymn of hope in the gods who give the unhoped for.

Yet it is possible to raise a first objection to this, and moreover one drawn from *Alcestis* itself. The unhoped for does not come according to hope; it is not the incandescent point of hope, inflamed by the divine in which we would have had confidence. If Alcestis returns to the shadows, this is because Heracles has snatched her away in hard battle with the gods of hell, in gratitude to Admetus for his friendship and hospitality, and not because Admetus would have continued to hope, in spite of everything and beyond all hope. What occurs does not bear any relationship with Admetus's hope or despair, if not indeed taking it by surprise. One could thus disclaim the lesson that it is necessary in every circumstance to hope in the divine power. Moreover, the same words close *Medea*, and at the end of this tragedy replete with violence and disorder there is a profound horror. The vision of a triumphant Medea, having accomplished her bloody and jubilant vengeance, before the bodies of her children that she has just assassinated, certainly does not put the unhoped for into play. In this passage, it would be correct to translate *aelptôs* as "unexpected." The word does not designate the fulfillment of a hope favored beyond what it could hope for, but the unforeseeable and disconcerting character of divine action in general, whether it has happy or disastrous consequences for us. This is a matter of an empty form that can be satisfied by either good or evil. Someone full of hope can see it

[8] *Alcestis* respectively 1123–1124, p. 275, and 1133–1134, p. 277.

crumble in unforeseeable horrors, and someone who is discouraged may see the arrival of joys that no one could have expected. This divine unexpected thus shines with an equivocal light, and it is normal that it is the least religious of the Greek tragedians who have displayed a special liking for such words by repeating them at the end of their works. The gesture is not so much toward confidence in the gods as toward the uncertainty of life and human knowledge.

The fact that what, from our human perspective, appears impossible does take place on divine initiative shows that every situation, even the best calculated, is susceptible to reversal, yet this does not mean that we can or must hope for the impossible, for our expectation and our hope are always determined by thoughts that are human, all too human. And the expression "hope for the unhoped for" has become, in Greece, a habitual locution for evoking a attitude that is unreasonable and heavy with illusion, in a manner similar to our contemporary expression: "ask for the impossible."[9] The unhoped for is not only what one *can* not hope for, but also what one *must* not hope for, on pain of sinking into derangement and puerility. On this expression and this common opinion, Heraclitus takes precisely the opposite position, and in one of the only places in Greek philosophy where the unhoped for, *to anelpiston*, is explicitly named in the absolute sense (fragment B18): "If you do not hope for the unhoped for, you will not find it. It is hard to find, and inaccessible."[10] From the moment that the possibility of hoping for the unhoped for becomes meaningful, the unhoped for could not be one among any number of objects of the hope

[9] Cf. K. Reinhardt, *Parmenides und die Geschichte der griechischen Philosophie* (Frankfurt: Klostermann, 1977), p. 63, following the determinations by Theodor Gomperz.

[10] According to enumeration by Diels-Kranz B18 / according to enumeration by Bywater 7. [English translation in consultation with C. Kahn, *Art and Thought of Heraclitus: An Edition of the Fragments with Translation and Commentary* (Cambridge: Cambridge University Press, 1981). Trans.] Diels is among those who punctuate differently, giving "If you do not hope, you will not find the unhoped for." But Gomperz has settled the question; cf. Reinhardt, op. cit., p. 63. [Many English translations render *anelpiston,* of capital importance throughout this book, as "unexpected," rather than Chrétien's "unhoped for." Trans].

characterizing an empirical situation that is, for example, critical or menacing. It becomes what defines the highest hope, a hope rendering all the others vain, in so far as it clears a path there where no path had hitherto been cleared and as if in expectation of our step. Hope disassociates itself from all calculation. It is the access to what is without access, the way toward the *aporon* as such. By this very fact, it turns us away from all other ways, from all the ways already cleared, as well as from that to which they conduct us: if one can hope for the unhoped for, is there anything else than this to truly hope for?

Just as the unforgettable requires payment in forgetting, and its light does not illumine without us having to separate what screens it, so the unhoped for, given to the fact of hoping, asks that we cease dispersing ourselves in a thousand hopes of every sort.[11] The unique hope for the unique wants to no longer fracture into multiple hopes. After all, as another statement from Heraclitus shows, to obtain everything that we hope for, when this hope is multiple, could produce a result wholly other than what we might think. "It is not good for men to get everything they wish."[12] Hoping for the unhoped for is so little an act of despair, or participates so little in an act of despair, that it is the ordinary attitude, in which one hopes only for the possible, and in which one hopes greatly for it, that is revealed to be miserable and dire. Such an ordinary hope does follow many paths, but they do not lead where one believes. Nothing establishes despair so well as false hopes, for they bear within their kaleidoscope, always and already, the mourning for a missing hope that is without image. What Heraclitus says of humanity is also true of our hope: "One is worth ten thousand, if it be the best."[13]

How are we to understand this hope for the unhoped for and this access to the inaccessible? Against Diels, who has asked

---

[11] This is said well by M. Conche, in his translation of Heraclitus, *Fragments* (Paris: Les belles lettres, 1986), p. 246: "What makes the philosopher is a hope wholly other than the multiple and worldly hopes common to mortals. . . . The philosopher renounces worldly conquests. In this regard, he hopes for nothing, or nothing more: to the hopes of non-philosophers is opposed the *unhope* of the philosopher."

[12] Diels-Kranz, B 110 (Bywater 104).

[13] Diels-Kranz, B 49 (Bywater 113).

whether this "hope" must be understood in the sense of the religions of mystery,[14] numerous commentators agree on its properly philosophical character and see truth and wisdom in the unhoped for, taking the view that it is in principle hidden from us.[15] From the moment that the unhoped for is considered unique, there can be no other meaning given to it. This being so, is it then necessary to reduce the paradox by saying that what *seems* impossible to many of us, and what, by the same stroke, one neither can nor should hope for, is the proper object of the philosophical desire that would discover its possibility? Is the unhoped for unhoped for only for illusion and opinion? The end of Fragment B18 prohibits this thought: what is said there is not that the unhoped for *seems* inaccessible, but that it *is* inaccessible. This is reinforced by the presence of two adjectives, "hard" and "inaccessible." And this is also precisely why we find the unhoped for only in hoping and in the one who hopes. Hoping goes out to meet what exceeds it by nature (and only hoping can do so, since it is purified). The superabundance of the unhoped for must not be diminished, and it has not at all mere semblance. Its light precedes us, it already passes through us, for the very act of hoping for the unhoped for, and thus of hoping otherwise and wholly other than most people hope; this act is itself already unhoped for. It presents an excess and a superabundance in relation to what one can expect from a human being. As for access to the inaccessible, this is no mere play on words.

The *unhoped for* is what transcends all our expectations, and the inaccessible is that to which no path takes us, whether it is one that is already traced or one that we project in thought. Encountering them would thus be the final step on a path or a course, in so far as it would be in continuity with what would

---

[14] Diels-Kranz, *Die Fragmente der Vorsokratiker,* 3 vols. (Zurich: Wiedman, 1989–1990, sixth edition), 1:155.

[15] Cf. Reinhardt, op. cit., p. 62: *"Nicht Mysterienhoffnung, sondern Erkenntnistheorie"* (even if this latter expression calls for some reservation); K. Held, *Heraklit, Parmenides und der Anfang von Philosophie und Wissenschaft, Eine phänomenologische Besinnung* (Berlin: de Gruyter, 1980), p. 332; M. Conche, op. cit., pp. 246–247.

precede it. When it emerges, the unhoped for necessarily has a sudden and discontinuous character. It surprises, since it has not been foreseen, anticipated, contained in advance by our thoughts. It strikes like lightning, all at once. But this does not mean that it is unnecessary for us to anticipate, because what cannot be anticipated meets us; and this does not mean that it is unnecessary for us to progress forward, because what lies outside all progress lays hold of us. Henry James's admirable and terrible story, "The Beast in the Jungle," shows what it costs to expect the unexpected in pure passivity. His character lives in the persuasion, which he interprets as a sign of election, that something absolutely unexpected will erupt into his existence. "Something or other lay in wait for him, amid the twists and the turns of the months and the years, like a crouching beast in the jungle. It signified little whether the crouching beast were destined to slay him or be slain. The definite point was the inevitable spring of the creature."[16] In consummating his life in the empty expectation of the unknown, he is blind to the true unhoped for, which remains quite close to him, in the love and fidelity of a woman who does not cease to accompany him. Hope for the unhoped for could not be such an empty horizon. Truth gives itself only to one who has loved it, even if its gifts transcend everything that we might expect. Anticipation of the unanticipatable is anticipation of the encounter that exposes us to alterity. This is why Heraclitus expresses himself in a negative formulation: "If you do not hope for the unhoped for, you will not find it." This supposes that one can indeed find it, and that the principle obstacle to doing so is not on its side, but on ours, in our absence of hope, in our renunciation, our withdrawal into our habitual preoccupations, where we seek only what we already know, in advance, what we can find without changing, without having to change.

An analogous access to the inaccessible is present in a thought wholly other than that of Heraclitus. In Plato's *Symposium*, the well ordered, patient, methodical path ascends toward

[16] H. James, "The Beast in the Jungle," in *Henry James. Complete Stories 1898–1910* (New York: Library of America, 1996), p. 508.

the vision of the Good fulfilled in sudden contemplation of it, and this suddenness is the gift of the unhoped for. If it is true that this sudden vision in which the Good itself shows itself completely is not our work, it is also true that it would not occur without work. Likewise, when Plotinus designates union with the One as issuing in a jump or leap, he shows its character to be sudden and unhoped for. But it is necessary to progress to a point where one must leap. To leap is to cross the void, to go where there is no path.[17] That said, one still wants to know: how could one reach—bit by bit, step by step, progressively—the place where it is no longer I who speak, but, through me, the Logos?[18] How could I pass little by little into an order wholly other than the one where I begin? No radical philosophy could ever make an economy of suddenness, of discontinuity, and thus none could ever dispense with hoping for the unhoped for. This unhoped for of philosophy has nothing in common with that of Euripides. It is at once closest to us and farthest,[19] since it is a matter of the Logos and truth. It is closest, for it is forever and does not cease to shine in the world. It is also farthest, for we are not awake to it.

However great the difference between these two Greek figures of the unhoped for, the one tragic and the other philosophical, they share the condition of not being open to the dimension of the promise. At the point where Revelation permits hope to become hope in God and confidence in God's promise, the unhoped for is charged with a new meaning. The hope in the unhoped for is thus the hope of Abraham. It is of him that St. Paul says, in the Epistle to the Romans, that "hoping against all hope he believed," returning to the promise of God.[20] Biblical hope has as its object what can be hoped for only

---

[17] Cf. our analyses in *La voix nue. Phénoménologie de la promesse* (Paris: Minuit, 1990), pp. 334–336, and "L'analogie selon Plotin," in *Les études philosophiques*, 3–4 (1989): 318.

[18] Heraclitus, B 50 (Bywater 1): "It is wise to listen not to me, but to my Word, and to know that all things are one."

[19] Cf. Heraclitus, B 72 (Bywater 93): "They are estranged from that with which they are in most common involvement"; and K. Held, op. cit., p. 332.

[20] Romans 4:18: *Hos par' elpida ep' elpidi episteusen, qui contra spem in spem credidit.*

from God, thus what is impossible by any human force, and what we neither could nor would have to hope for from ourselves and by ourselves. There, too, though again in a wholly different sense than in philosophy, hope renounces what one ordinarily regards as hope. Philo of Alexandria has made the sudden and unhoped for character of divine gifts the center of his thinking. The same example that St. Paul takes up in his Epistle to the Romans—the birth of Isaac to an Abraham who is one hundred years old and a Sara who is sterile—is frequently also his. When God promises this lineage, "Abraham," says the book of Genesis, "fell on his face and laughed."[21] Philo comments on this verse as follows: "Two things can befall a sage at the same time, when he is granted goods exceeding his hope *(meizona elpidos agatha):* he laughs and he falls to the earth. He falls as a pledge that he takes no pride from this, having seen the nothingness of mortality; he laughs to reaffirm his piety before God, judging that God is the unique cause of graces and good things."[22] This two seemingly inverse movements—humiliation and uplifting, dejection and exaltation—constitute the space in which the unhoped for is received: together they signify that the unhoped for is not and cannot be our work, they recognize and confess its excessive character. And the thought of the unhoped for goes together with the thought of humility. Philo's treatise on Abraham returns to this same example: "Much later, a legitimate son was born to those who had despaired of having children: this reward for their virtue, more perfect than anything one could hope for *(elpidos pasès teleioteron),* they had been given by the generous God."[23] Some lines prior to that, Philo, praising Sara, insists on her care for the future and her foresight. But what is given to her does not come from this: she is given a future that they could not have expected, hoped for, or produced.

[21] Genesis 17:17.

[22] Philo of Alexandria, *De mutatione nominum,* 155. *Philo of Alexandria,* vol. 5, trans. F. H. Colson and G. H. Whitaker (Cambridge: Harvard/Loeb, 1934), pp. 222–224.

[23] Philo, *De Abrahamo,* 254. *Philo of Alexandria,* vol. 4, trans. F. H. Colson (Cambridge: Harvard/Loeb, 1935), p. 125.

Philo emphasizes the suddenness with which the unhoped for is given, as well as its power of renewal. He reprises the Platonic verb *exaiphnès,* but also loves to use *exapinaiôs,* which means, equally, *sudden (soudain), suddenly (subitement), all at once,* and *unexpectedly.*[24] It is again with regard to Abraham that the radical newness of the unhoped for is evoked: "It has also been said that one must 'clear away the old to make way for the new.' Such a need of the timeworn and of old and outdated customs is still present in those on whom is lavished all at once, without them expecting it *(expinaiôs ou prosdokèsasin),* a shower of new and incomparable goods."[25] Abraham remembers the promise and remains faithful to the unforgettable in going out to meet the unhoped for, leaving everything that is timeworn. If one must offer God the first fruits, if "the holy word teaches persuasively that one is to occupy oneself with what is new and with all the freshness of a blossoming youth," this is because at the very heart of the created, newness furnishes an image of God and his action. Mythology delights in the evocation of the very old, whereas biblical faith loves what is new. In order to represent divine power, "timeless and instantaneous," what comes rightly from birth and awakening offers better images than do the deep past and the abysses of the immemorial. In God, "there is nothing old, and nothing at all past,"[26] says Philo. The fate of Lot's wife, petrified while turning back toward Sodom, symbolizes the life arrested by fascination with the ancient, blind to the perpetual newness of the divine.[27] This newness is sudden, instantaneous, and time has nothing to do with it, for by itself, says Philo, it does nothing.[28]

---

[24] Which is found once, under the form *exapina,* in the Gospel of Mark, 9:8, at the end of the Transfiguration narrative.

[25] Philo, *Quis rerum divinarum heres sit,* 279. The scriptural reference is to Leviticus 26:10. [This text is not included in the Loeb translations; English translates Crétien's French. Trans.]

[26] Philo, *De sacrificiis Abelis et Caini,* 76. *Philo of Alexandria,* vol. 2, trans. F. H. Colson and G. H. Whitaker (Cambridge: Harvard/Loeb, 1929), pp. 151–153.

[27] Philo, *De ebrietate,* 164. *Philo of Alexandria,* vol. 3, trans. F. H. Colson and G. H. Whitaker (Cambridge: Harvard/Loeb, 1930), p. 403.

[28] Philo, *De sacrificiis Abelis et Caini,* 77. *Philo of Alexandria,* trans. Colson and Whitaker, 2:153.

He also frequently opposes the goods produced by our pain, sweat, and labor with the goods given from God. These latter, "which, outside of any art and in general any human project, spring up independently and are born immediately, beyond even hope of reaching them,"[29] can only be given. Philo refers to this wisdom that one learns by oneself, spontaneously, without recourse and with no other master than God himself, as "autodidactic." When it is given to us, "we must straightaway *(euthus)* exclude and eradicate the knowledge that comes to us from teaching," the knowledge that is subject to being damaged and lost.[30] There again, the old and the new must be separated, inasmuch as each comes under a different order, and indeed Philo cites the verse in Leviticus that prescribes making the old disappear in the face of the new. As opposed to what we learn of the past and faithfully preserve in memory, Philo speaks of the "sudden light" that "shines for those who did not foresee it and did not hope for it."[31]

The birth of Isaac is a radiant manifestation of the unhoped for.[32] But Isaac himself, son of the promise, becomes for Philo the symbol par excellence of "autodidactic" wisdom, that is to say wisdom to which God alone introduces us, and which one finds without having sought it. To be sure, it frequently happens that, regarding the unhoped for and the Isaac who represents it, Philo speaks of what is given by God "to those who seek."[33] But more frequently, he says that the highest moment of the spiritual life is one of finding without seeking. A long section of *De fuga et inventione* thus distinguishes between four types of people in function of their respective relations to search and discovery: those who do not seek and do not find, those who seek and find, those who seek without finding, and those who find without seeking.[34] This last category is by far the most ele-

---

[29] Philo, *De mutatione nominum,* 219. *Philo of Alexandria,* trans. Colson and Whitaker, 5:257.

[30] Philo, *De sacrificiis Abelis et Caini,* 79; 2:155.

[31] Ibid., 78; 2:153. "Sudden light" translates *pheggos aiphnidion.* Philo uses all of the Greek words for suddenness.

[32] Philo, *De mutatione nominum,* 218; 5:255.

[33] Ibid., 269; 5:279.

[34] Philo, *De fuga et inventione,* 120f. *Philo of Alexandria,* vol. 5, trans. F. H. Colson and G. H. Whitaker (Cambridge: Harvard/Loeb, 1934), pp. 75f.

vated: "It is there that we find every wise man who gets his knowledge and instruction from himself *(automathès kai autodidaktos).*" It is comes "not by human design but in a God-inspired ecstasy *(entheôi maniai).*"[35] By itself it is new and vivid. "Thus, the knowledge that one acquires demands a great deal of time, but the knowledge that one gets from nature is rapid *(takhu)* and, in a sense, timeless *(akhronon).* Man serves as the guide for one; God, for the other."[36] From his very birth, Isaac represents it.

Suddenness makes up a part of the essence of this gift, rather then being no more than a circumstance. It confers on the gift the character of encounter. This encounter can be completely unforeseen, not being provoked by us and not resulting from any search or labor on our part, but it does not occur without desire or hope. In this respect, Philo could borrow Heraclitus's statement about hope for the unhoped for. For him, too, the unhoped for comes only to those who hope for it. But if it is nonetheless true that he thinks of the unhoped for in a different manner, and more forcefully, this is in order to inscribe hope for God in the very definition of humanity. This is the site of a significant philosophical revolution misunderstood by those who, reducing Philo to his lectures, find only what they were looking for, which is to say what they already knew. "In reality, is there anything more proper to those of us who are truly human, than the hope and expectation where one possesses the goods that only the generous God can give?" For Philo, to lose hope is to forfeit our humanity. Far from being a misleading passion, one that generates illusion, hope forms the very heart of our being. This is to define our humanity by its future, and to make of our being a relation with the Other. "The composite definition of what we are would thus be: a rational mortal animal subject to death; but according to Moses what defines us is the disposition of a soul hoping in the God who really is."[37] This

[35] Ibid., respectively 166 (5:101) and 168 (5:101), *entheôi maniai.* Philo reprises the Platonic words for divine madness.

[36] Ibid., 169; 5:103.

[37] Philo, *Quod deterius potiori insidiari soleat,* 139–140. *Philo of Alexandria,* vol. 2, trans. F. H. Colson and G. H. Whitaker (Cambridge: Harvard/Loeb, 1929), p. 295.

represents a profound reversal of Greek thinking about human nature, which is stricken forever and without return, if not unto despair, by the lack of what is radically new. The unhoped for calls to our hope, claiming us at the most intimate level of ourselves.

The fact that this would have the character of encounter is registered in an admirable phrase from *De somniis*: "The divine Word, appearing unexpectedly *(exapinaiôs)*, like a fellow traveler for the soul that walks alone, brings it a joy that is unexpected and surpasses all hope."[38] Expressed in Greek with a verb, the beautiful comparison with a fellow traveler underlines the fact that the suddenness of divine gifts has nothing fleeting about it. What comes in the instant and can only come in the instant, and comes without preparation and without prehistory; but by its interruption it opens a new time, a newness that does not pass and renews us ceaselessly. Only the sudden can initiate an epoch. As a metaphor for the unhoped for, the notion of a treasure found by chance shows that in reality the only treasure is the unhoped for itself, which escapes those who seek. "Oftentimes there befalls us what we would not have envisioned beforehand, even in a dream; like the laborer in the fable, who dug into the earth in order to plant some fruit trees, and came upon a treasure, joyously unhoped for *(anelpistôi eutukhiai)*." What one finds quickly, says Philo, is what God gives us. "For when God makes a gift to us of the precepts of eternal wisdom, we find all at once *(exaiphnès)*, without fatigue or labor, without expecting it, the treasure of perfect bliss."[39] This is the joy of light, as unhoped for as it is unforgettable, and of the trait evoked in order to oppose people of labor and strife with those who, waking from a deep sleep and merely opening their eyes, "suddenly *(exaiphnès)* discover the world, without trouble or active effort."[40] As Malebranche has put it, perfect knowledge

---

[38] Philo, *De somniis,* I, 71. *Philo of Alexandria,* vol. 5, trans. F. H. Colson and G. H. Whitaker (Cambridge: Harvard/Loeb, 1934), pp. 333–335.

[39] Philo, *Quod Deus sit immutabilis,* 91–92. *Philo of Alexandria,* vol. 3, trans. F. H. Colson and G. H. Whitaker (Cambridge: Harvard/Loeb, 1930), p. 57.

[40] Ibid., 97; 3:59.

of optics and geometry would not be enough for them to give themselves this sudden vision of a countryside.[41] They receive it, and it surpasses anything that they could produce. What is seized in a single blink of the eye, no amount of searching could enable them to expect. The instant of the gift brings together the unforgettable and the unhoped for, in the gratuity of excess. To find without seeking is to let oneself find without having held the initiative. And letting oneself find is endless when it is God who does the finding.

The cult of the search for its own sake, of the search that would be worthwhile in itself even if it would find nothing, is the mark of diversion in Pascal's sense, in which one "loves the chase better than the quarry."[42] In this line, Lessing's famous parable on the search for truth can be considered to have something idolatrous in it. Lessing imagines that God gives him a choice between full knowledge of the truth, to be granted to him by God, and perpetual movement toward the truth "even with the supplementary condition of being always and eternally mistaken." Thus, he says, "out of a humility" that sets aside for God alone the possession of the truth, he would decide only for the undefined quest.[43] How could love of the truth never love to encounter it? And the alleged "humility" which prefers seeking to receiving substitutes the egocentric and derisory enjoyment of our own procedures, passions, and feelings for the truth itself. This is to enter into an idolatry of self. It forgets that the truth given by God, even if given suddenly, needs an eternity to be received, for receiving is also an endless task, and receiving what does not cease is itself ceaseless. In renouncing the unhoped for, according to the thinking that says we could not be its author, Lessing also renounces hope, and his parable thus represents the perfect inverse of what is said in Heraclitus's statement on the unhoped for. To know how to hope is to know how to be unable to attain by oneself what one hopes for, and

[41] Malebranche, *Entretien d'un philosophe chrétien et d'un philosophe chinois, Œuvres complètes,* vol. 15 (Paris: Pléiade, 1970), pp. 14–15.

[42] Pascal, *Pensées,* § 139.

[43] Lessing's parable is cited in J. Colette, *Histoire et absolu* (Paris: Vrin, 1972), p. 174.

thus also to learn ceaselessly to receive. As a thinker of the unhoped for, Philo of Alexandria relates, in a rare page where he speaks in the first person, how he encountered it even in philosophical reflection. The thought of the unhoped for can itself be unhoped for thought. Philo describes the powerlessness and sterility of his efforts on some days, and how, at other times, when he felt empty and unable to search, he was "all at once *(exaiphnès)* filled with ideas falling widely, and invisibly sown from above, "like snow."[44]

The correlation of the sudden, of what takes place once and for all, with the unforgettable and the unhoped for characterizes all thought of the promise. It is at the heart of all biblical theology. It can also be rediscovered, but transposed, weakened, and equivocal, when our promise takes the place of God's promise. And Kant places it at the center of his morality. As moral subjects, we are unexpected by ourselves. Analyzing moral formation, the "Methodology of Pure Practical Reason" opposes the play of fear and interest to the presentation of the "pure moral motive," the categorical imperative, without either extortion or seduction. It alone can be the "ground of character" and leads us to found our own. It alone can also give to the soul "a power unexpected even by oneself, to pull oneself loose from all sensuous attachments," making us discover our own dignity.[45] In becoming ourselves, we surprise ourselves and grasp resources in ourselves that nothing could have led us to suspect were there. Only the law, and the solemn recognition of our autonomy, reveals them to us. The *Anthropology from a Pragmatic Point of View* insists on the suddenness of the foundation of character, a suddenness that is always epoch-making. Character is not received from nature, but given to us from ourselves. The sole thing that we can give ourselves is a promise, which is to say a future. The foundation of character, says Kant, is like a "rebirth" *(Wiedergebeurt),* and this expression aptly expresses the fact that it is like a moral baptism that one confers on oneself. It has

---

[44] Philo, *De migratione Abrahami,* 35. *Philo of Alexandria,* vol. 4, trans. F. H. Colson and G. H. Whitaker (Cambridge: Harvard/Loeb, 1932), p. 151.

[45] I. Kant, *Critique of Practical Reason,* trans. L. W. Beck (New York: MacMillan, 1993), p. 158.

"this solemnity of the vow that one makes to oneself," and "the instant in which this condition is produced in a man immediately makes a new epoch for him unforgettable *(unvergesslich).*" Nothing of this sort can occur little by little or progressively, but only through a sort of "explosion," produced "all at once" *(auf einmal)* by our distaste at the fluttering of instinct, as it leads us like its playthings from one side to another.[46]

This solitary baptism of autonomy transposes the traits of a true baptism—always received from the other—within the limits of ethical reason alone, and it could not lead to a strong sense of the unhoped for. It is noteworthy that in theology the word *character* designates the imprint left in us by the divine action working through the sacrament of baptism and through its order, whereas for Kant it is the rule of our actions that give us to ourselves. We cannot and could not receive anything. Kant pushes the object of hope back to infinity, since the immortality postulated by pure practical reason, in a purely philosophical manner, consists only in pursuing the effort to become holy beyond death, without end. The creature "cannot hope here or at any foreseeable point of his future existence to be fully adequate to God's will."[47] It would be absurd and immoral to hope for the unhoped for, that is to say, grace. We will have to content ourselves with a fate of consolation, and for all of that one that is totally extrinsic: in his unique timeless intuition, God will regard our perfection without end, as well as—as Hegel has shown, and as the equivalent of our perfection—our imperfection without end. God looks, and gives nothing. His very gaze does not form a gift, since it keeps only to its eternal nature, and not to his love. But could I make myself reborn to myself, inaugurating this infinite progress, more than I have given birth to myself the first time? Is every promise that I give given only to myself, before the law of which I am at once the legislator and the subject? Is the unforgettable of my promise without

---

[46] I. Kant, *Anthropologie im pragmatischen Hinsicht,* in *Werke,* vol. 8 (Darmstadt: Suhrkamp, 1983), p. 655 (*Akademie Textausgabe*, vol. 7, p. 294).

[47] Kant, *Critique of Practical Reason*, p. 130.

past? And does the suddenness of this vow, opening a future previously impossible, make appeal only to itself, or does it respond to an appeal that has been addressed to it—does it respond to the promise that always sends us?

In his third letter, as brief as it is decisive, Dionysius the Areopagite, referring to a statement from the prophet Malachi,[48] understands the sudden, the *exaiphnès,* in the incarnation of Christ. "Sudden is what comes against all hope and thus passes from shadow to light. As for what concerns Christ's love of men, I believe theology uses this term to indicate that the hyper-essential has gone out from its secret and become manifest to us in assuming a human essence. But it is also secret beyond this manifestation, or rather, to speak in more divine fashion, in this manifestation itself."[49] Revelation does not abolish mystery, but reveals mystery as such. It is turned toward us without ceasing to be the mystery of God. What is against all hope, radically unhoped for, is that the depth of divine life, itself absolutely hidden from the thinking that is at grips with man, is manifest to us. Divine *philanthropia* gives itself to see and to love, completely and in all suddenness, in the Incarnation. The unhoped for founds, and because it has taken on a face, it does not cease to be unhoped for from the moment it has taken place. Sacred history is fulfilled in the full revelation of the Holy itself, and the flash of its suddenness bears in it all the depth of time. We are not inclined toward the unhoped for as toward a distant future, for the unhoped for has been given, it has a place and a date. Yet, notwithstanding that, this accomplished unhoped for does not become the object of a simple retrospection. It absolutely founds the future in so far as it has taken place. The faithful exist from the unhoped for, and only the unhoped for gives hope and founds it. The cross unfolds and reunites the dimensions of time. It assembles the history of the promise in keeping it, and in still promising it.

---

[48] Dionysius the Areopagite, *Malachie*, III, 1.

[49] *Exaiphnès esti to par'elpida,* in *Patrologia grecque,* Migne, III, 1069 B. Translated by M. de Gaudillac. *Œuvres complètes* de Pseudo-Denys (Paris: Montaigne, 1980), pp. 328–329. Cf. our book, *Lueur du secret* (Paris: Eds. de L'Herne, 1985).

The fact that God remains *kruphios,* secret, in his very manifestation, and that revelation reveals his excess over our speech and our thought,[50] ensures that the unhoped for does not cease at any instant to be unhoped for and to come to us with a disruptive suddenness. Our hope could not be so sure that the gift that it hopes for exceeds us and exceeds all human hope, unless this gift had already been made to that hope, and unless the promise that we receive has already been kept. The place where God gives his promise is already the place where he keeps it; the place where he keeps it is still the place where he gives it. What more, after all, could God give than Himself? "He who has seen me has seen the Father," says Christ to Philip.[51] In so far as faith hopes, it is sent and thrown to the extremities of time by the promises of God that it has charge of not forgetting. God's promise unites the immemorial, unforgettable, and unhoped for. The genesis is immemorial, for we were not there when God founded the earth, and the origin is always already a past for us, forgotten without return. Through the word of God, this immemorial becomes unforgettable, for the sacred history that we must always remember begins with creation itself. This remembrance of the impossible is anticipation and this memory is hope, for in the Bible praise for the creator God is not separated from praise for the savior God.[52] Recalling the origin belongs properly to hope tending toward its end. But this hope in God does not anticipate emptily, for it is in remembering the unhoped for given in grace to our fathers and mothers and to us, and in remembering what exceeds human heart and vision, that one still and always hopes. Uniting memory and hope, the book of Deuteronomy speaks of the promise of the earth itself, with its cities that you (Israel) have not built, houses that you have not stocked, cisterns that you have not hewn, and vineyards and olive trees that you have not planted.[53] This is a matter

[50] Cf. the end of Dionysius's Letter III: "Even said, it remains unsayable, even thought, it remains unknowable."

[51] John 14:9.

[52] Cf. the forceful analyses of G. von Rad, in his *Old Testament Theology*, 2 vols. (London: SCM Press, 1975).

[53] Deuteronomy 6:10–12.

of the unhoped for, and in these words Philo of Alexandria saw the very signature of divine gifts, beyond every expectation and all human effort. He understands the vine as the symbol of joy, and the olive as that of light.[54] For its oil does not only nourish, but also clarifies, like speech. In the patient darkness of the olive, there matures the seed of future brightness. How could we have planted such a tree? And how could we remember anything but this promise, which must make us forget everything? In the quiet of the night, there is always already, always again, for those who hope in remembering and remember in hoping, for those who keep watch—there is to be heard from afar, wounding us in our most secret depths, the soft and lissom rustle of the passing wind, whose gentle touch blesses the olive tree.

[54] Philo, *De fuga et inventione,* 175–176; 5:105–107, and *Quod Deus sit immutabilis,* 96; 3:59.

RETROSPECTION

IT HAS SEEMED opportune to the author of this book, a dozen years after having written it, and on the occasion of this new edition, to situate it in the philosophical and spiritual path of which it is not the first moment and which is pursued still today, so as to clarify for the reader the general project in which it finds a place.

In the meditation on memory found in Book X of the *Confessions,* St. Augustine shows, in expressions that Heidegger judged decisive, that he who interrogates the capacities of human nature transforms himself by himself into an interrogation: "I have become a question to myself."[1] And it is in fact this question that brings him truly to wonder at himself: "I have become for myself a soil which is cause of difficulty and much sweat," for "I cannot grasp the totality of what I am."[2] This almost unbearable test that a person becomes for himself is related not at all to evil or sin, but to the excess of a human being over himself, an excess of what one is and can be over what one can think and comprehend. It is in this sense that St. Augustine qualifies the force of the memory of "I know not what horror" *(nescio quid horrendum),* such that it assuredly bears no evil.[3] What is this excess, and what are we to think of this overflowing or transcendence of self over itself?

This is about the world, about Being and God, about everything that a person is through being *exposed.* It has to do with everything to which one must respond through the word, that is to say everything, all the way to nothing. It is about what is

[1] Augustine, *Confessions* X, xxxiii, 50, trans. H. Chadwick (Oxford: Oxford University Press, 1991), p. 208. [Chadwick translates: "problem to myself". Trans.]

[2] Augustine, *Confessions* X, xvi, 25, p. 193, and X, vii, 15, p. 187.

[3] *Confessions* X, xvii, 26.

given to a person, the gift to which one is opened without recourse, about being the only one who can say *Me voici,* here I am, and having said it already, even in silence, by one's face, hands, and entire body. "It is movement that does not speak," writes Montaigne.[4] The first page of Paul Claudel's *Tête d'Or* admirably shows this rise of man to the world, in a trembling of both uncertainty and ardor at the same time, and in a great abeyance of all possibilities:

> *Me voici*
> *Imbécile, ignorant*
> *Homme nouveau devant les choses inconnues*
> *Qu'est-ce que je fais? Qu'est-ce que j'attends?*
> *Et je réponds: Je ne sais pas! Et je désire en moi-même*
> *Pleurer, ou crier,*
> *Ou rire, ou bondir et agiter les bras!*[5]
> [*Here I am*
> *Imbecile, ignorant*
> *New man before unknown things*
> *What do I do? What do I expect?*
> *And I reply: I do not know! And I desire within myself*
> *To weep, or cry out*
> *Or laugh, or leap and wave my arms!*]

These are thus entirely one thing: the question that he is to himself, the question that he poses to the world, and the question that the world poses to him.

The French say of someone who regains understanding after falling unconscious that he has come back to himself. But to come back to oneself is to open one's eyes again in order to exist once again in relation with others and the world; to come back to oneself is therefore to take leave of oneself in order to live in the "common world" of which Heraclitus writes, leaving the tenebrous immanence of darkness for the Open. Meditating on the latter, Henri Maldiney says of existence that "it is open only in opening itself to the event in the surprise of reality." And he adds, "Man would not speak if he did not have a thirst for

---

[4] Montaigne, *Essais*, II, 12, (Paris: Gallimard, 1962), p. 431.
[5] P. Claudel, *Théâtre*, vol. 1, (Paris: Pléiade, 1967), pp. 171–172.

everything."[6] No one testifies to this better than William Faulkner, in a letter devoid of affectation: "I am telling the same story over and over, which is myself and the world," and in other words their meeting in the event which would be for him the advent of the world. That this was not in any way a matter of autobiography is attested in this same correspondence by Faulkner's wish to be annihilated as an individual in human memory, to leave no other trace than his books, and of having as his biography only the following: "He made the books, and he died"[7]—a would-be biography close to the one Heidegger in fact did give to Aristotle.

But how to say everything? How to respond to what is properly excessive and inordinate in relation to all our possibilities in the encounter with the world? In writing of the impossible, in taking the word to say everything, each time (by which Faulkner confesses himself to be a *poet*, in the end, more than in his poems): "I'm trying to say it all in one sentence, between one cap and one period. I'm still trying to put it all, if possible, on one pinhead. All I know to do is keep on trying in a new way."[8] All true writing has something inchoate in it.

It is this *excess* of the encounter with things, other, world, and God that is at the center of the project of which this book is a part: this encounter requires, most imperatively, our response, and yet seems at the same to prohibit it. Different figures of this excess have been tackled in successive works. In *l'Effoi de beau* (1987),[9] a work on the encounter itself, it is, as the title indicates, beauty—a beauty properly arresting, and reaching our existence at its heart—which was put into play, or rather which put the book into play. Beauty torn from the profanations of aesthetics and described as "pure event," according to an expression from Valéry, in the light of Plato and

[6] H. Maldiney, *L'art, l'éclair de l'être* (Paris: Eds. Comp' act, 1993), pp. 96 and 99.

[7] Malcolm Cowley, *The Faulkner-Cowley Files. Letters and Memories. 1944–1962* (New York: Viking, 1966), pp. 14 and 126.

[8] Ibid., p. 14.

[9] [Complete information on Chrétien's books can be found at the end of this volume. Trans.]

Rilke.[10] The relation to beauty is understood there as an *existential*, an essential dimension of human existence. The joy with which beauty strikes us delivers us to word and song, to thanks and praise, but how could the response to it not fall short of it? This question leads to two theses that the following works have not ceased to deepen. To begin with, the way the response falls short constitutes neither a contingent deficit nor a regrettable imperfection in the response that we give to the manifestation of the beautiful that occurs in the form of a request. It is the very event of a wound by which our existence is altered and opened, and becomes itself the site of the manifestation of what it responds to. There is true force only in weakness, a weakness that is opened up by what comes toward us. The fact that the wound can bless and that benediction can wound are the locus of meditations at the heart of *Corps à corps* (1997), concerning Jacob's struggle with the angel. This comes down to thinking finitude positively, as the place where there can truly be—though not transparently—a testimony to the infinite. At the same time, the way the response to beauty falls short of beauty invokes, by essential necessity, chorus and polyphony: the response accomplishes its unsubstitutable singularity only in giving itself into a community and thus making appeal to other voices. This is not because they complete that response, but because the fault is closed only at the same time as our mouths.

Taking up the particular theme of "night" in poetry, *l'Antiphonaire de la nuit* (1989) is also a direct continuation of this meditation. The term *antiphonary* evokes simultaneously a word that is essentially response (here, "night"), and speech that is essentially choral.[11] In an implicit manner, though at certain points unmistakable to some, and made explicit in *l'Appel et la réponse* (1992), this was a critique of Heidegger on speech

[10] Readers in the medical field will have truly understood what this beauty is, from having seen a smile transfigure the face of people suffering grave illness, or whose illness has devastated their features. Like "grace" for Plotinus, beauty does not belong to the face, as one of its properties, but comes to it, or takes place there.

[11] [The English word "antiphonary" generally refers to the Christian "Divine Office," in which Psalms and canticles are sung or recited in responsive alternation between groups within a community. Trans.]

as correspondence *(Entsprechung),* since this is one aspect of the concept of a falling-short in the response. To criticize Heidegger is always virtually presumptuous, above all when it is a matter of a work as extraordinarily incisive as *On the Way to Language,* a work, moreover, from a thinker who is himself extraordinary among his contemporaries—but what path worth taking does not also involve some risk? The study of nocturnal poetry would seem to show above all the responsive nature of speech, since this poetry tends always to become vocative, to address itself to the night. But what is this "night"? The night is already other: a number of poetic works observe a doubling of night, affirming two distinct nights—though, of course, according to diverse distinctions. This leads one to think of words as *translation:* speech translates, it crosses from what befalls it over to what it addresses—in this case, from the night that falls on it to the night that is addressed. This translation is the very process of our alteration by what strikes us, the movement in which the distinction between appeal and response is erased. Marina Tsvetaieva said: "To write poems is already to translate,"[12] something that Novalis had already thought. This paradox of an originary translation belongs to the rigorous description of a phenomenology of response. In an analysis dedicated to the night of the origin and the night of the end, this book opened the meditation on excess to a meditation on time: "Each night that we pass, that we cross from one day to the other, is at once recall and call *(rappel et appel),* re-memoration and anticipation, re-memoration of the beginning and anticipation of the end. It does not recall us to an object of memory, but rather to what founds all memory and its condition, it does not call us to an object of expectation, but to the extremity that permits it and orients it." It was a question, there, of what "exceeds all memory and thereby founds re-memoration" and of what "exceeds all expectation, and thereby founds anticipation."[13] These ques-

[12] [An English translation of this passage from Madame Tsvetaeva appears on the first page of J. Bayley's "Introduction" to R. M. Rilke, *Selected Letters. 1902–1926* (London: Quartet Books, 1988), trans. R. F. C. Hull, p. xiii. Trans.]

[13] J.-L. Chrétien, *L'Antiphonaire de la nuit* (Paris: Eds. de L'Herne, 1989), p. 75.

tions are already those of the book republished here, *The Unforgettable and the Unhoped For.*

The acute point of the present and of our presence takes its acuity only from its encounter with the inordinate extremities of a time that is not ours, but also the way the whole of humanity encounters the One who calls it to itself, and the way each of us encounters a past more ancient than all memory and a future beyond all expectation. This vision appears bottomless: nonetheless, it is what confronts us each time that we take speech. The speech that renders present the past and the future, that makes present the absent, is also that without which the present does not rise up and take form. This is why any meditation on time that is not also a meditation on the word is futile. Now this speech that we take up is received from other people who have received it themselves without possibility of seeing it appear, just as we transmit it to others who will transmit it without possibility of seeing it disappear. This does not amount to saying that humanity has not had a beginning and could not have an end, but to saying that it makes no sense to specify what there is when we no longer are, or not yet are, unless it is to transport ourselves there, by speech itself, as fictive witnesses, and thus to act as if we are already there, or still are there. This double ungraspable horizon of speech is the primary human form taken by the question of the extremities of time, of the *eskhata.* Henri Maldiney's existentials of *transpossibility* and *transpassability*—evoking, respectively, a power and a suffering irreducible to any system of possibles[14]—could contribute to describing the relation to these extremities.

Every present worthy of the name is agonistic; it is torn by an unsustainable tension, and this is why it is present. There is an event only for the one who can not only promise (according to Nietzsche's definition of man), but can promise and also receive the promises of others, which to say can engage himself *forever.* The event is what makes possible this *forever* that would otherwise be impossible, and this alone is why there is, by way of

[14] Cf. H. Maldiney, *Penser l'homme et la folie* (Grenoble: Jerôme Millon, 1991), pp. 421 and 81.

consequence, a *no longer* as things were before. Under the heading of "the event," one could not think a capricious freedom enchanted with its own plasticity and amazed at seeing itself changed by what comes to it in a play of adventures that is both kaleidoscopic and, ultimately, aesthetic. For the only response to the event is not simply to change or be changed, be it quite profoundly, but to found and open an interminable future—failing which, the event could be said to also concern animals and plants. The promise is the only event where we receive more than we can receive, by opening all the future to receive it. It is in this sense that Karl Rahner says that "freedom is the capacity to do something final and definitive."[15]

l'Effroi de beau has shown that the excess of the beautiful over our gaze and voice is what gives our song, in so far as it is wounded through and through, its humanity and incandescence. *l'Appel et la réponse* has shown that the excess of the appeal over our response, in so far as it crosses this response through and through, is what gives it its stature and weight. *The Unforgettable and the Unhoped For* makes this same attempt with time: the excess of the immemorial and the unhoped for over our present, in so far as they tear it apart from one end to the other, is what gives to the present its precariousness and its splendid luster. These diverse works have also attempted to show that certain themes that contemporary thought has sometimes believed itself to initiate are in fact already present and alive in the ancient traditions. For religious and mystical thought and speech have frequently seen and spoken higher, farther, or otherwise than metaphysics in the form that Heidegger has defined for us. And it is necessary to hear their promises. For they are not obsessed and blinded by the human project of total self-assurance and self-understanding as we truly are (to paraphrase St. Paul), in transparency: they are rooted at each instant in the hearing of an other Word that wounds body and soul, and which they know that, if it wounds completely, could never be completely understood—not even in eternity. This is

[15] K. Rahner, *Foundations of Christian Faith*, trans. W. Dych (New York: Crossroad, 1978), p. 96.

why religious and mystical thought and speech are necessary for those who would meditate on excess and superabundance, on the force in weakness and the perfection in deficiency. They do more than speak of them; they live them and originate from them.

Through the course of some years, the various essays gathered into *la Voix nue, Phénoménologie de la promesse* (1990) prepared more unitary formulations. The titles of its two sections, "Critique de la transparence" and "La passé de la promesse," indicate some general dimensions, as much negative as positive. Under the name "transparence" are isolated some forms of thought where manifestation will have lost the luster of its secret, and thus by the same stroke its depth and weight—where presence would be plenary and glorious but therefore also without future, where speech would like to be first and last, the total master of the meaning that it institutes. It is a matter of thinking loss, wound, and passivity, as well as forgetting and fatigue, which are phenomena where the trace of the excessive shines through, outside the idealistic and dialectical language of "negativity" in which everything is as if vanquished and surmounted in advance. There is no philosophical parousia.

In this field of thought, *l'Appel et la réponse* forms a decisive stage. It will be not only in philosophy, as some would have it, but also outside of it that the responsive nature of the word and thus of human presence is deepened. One thinks, in this sense, of Heidegger meditating on the Hölderlin's statement "We are a dialogue," and writing "Dialogue is not only a way in which language is accomplished, but it is also uniquely as dialogue that language is essential."[16] One thinks too of Mikhail Bakhtine affirming that this was his central theme: "The expression of a spoken *(un énoncé)* is always, to a greater or lesser degree, a *response.*"[17] Or of Virginia Woolf saying, in one of her novels: "Was not writing poetry a secret transaction, a voice answering a voice?" A naked voice that responds not only to other human

---

[16] M. Heidegger, Gesamtausgabe, vol. 39, *Hölderlins Hymnen "Germanien" und "Der Rhein"* (Frankfurt: Klostermann, 1980), pp. 68, 69.

[17] M. Bakhtine, *Esthétique de la création verbale* (Paris: Gallimard, 1984), p. 299.

voices, but to the visible voice of themselves: "What could have been more secret, she thought, more slow, and like the intercourse of lovers, than the stammering answer she had made all these years to the old crooning song of the woods, and the farms and the brown horses standing at the gate, neck to neck, and the smithy and the kitchen and the fields, so laboriously bearing wheat, turnips, grass, and the gardens blowing irises and fritillaries."[18] It is clear that neither intersubjectivity nor inter-textuality could make all of this thinkable. But it was more decisive for this work to have shown that the *body*, as unique bearer of speech, is the very site of any response to the appeal. This is what founds the central character of *voice, breath,*[19] and *nudity:* this will not be the speech of angels! (Need it be added, however, that it is precisely in this place that there is articulated, in this same philosophical project, another voice and another field—poetic—to explore these phenomena?[20]).

This thought of the body as *responding* has since been at the heart of the book *De la fatigue* (1996)[21] and the essays in *Corps à corps, A l'écoute de l'oeuvre de l'art* (1997), which opens it to forms of response that are other than verbal. It is also a matter of thinking the historicity of this response, and thus of the body itself. Of the body, Paul Claudel has spoken with such profound accuracy that there is no further need to endorse each detail: "We are not like a soldier on his horse or a sailor in his boat, but like a laborer in his work and the flame in its torch. This is what makes us, this is our expression as a word, the form that we give to the exterior, the reality of our presence, our way of responding to the call of God and of furnishing him with a likeness."[22] It is a matter of thinking *how* the body can be this response.

---

[18] V. Woolf, *Orlando* (New York: Harcourt Brace, 1956), p. 325.

[19] [Chrétien's word *souffle,* rendered here as "breath," can also signify "inspiration." Trans.]

[20] This has been seen by Jérôme de Gramont. Cf. his *L'entrée en philosophie* (Paris: L'Harmattan, 1999), p. 68, for another presentation of this line of thought.

[21] Cf. J.-L. Chrétien, *De la fatigue* (Paris: Eds. de Minuit, 1996), p. 15, and *l'Appel et la réponse* (Paris: Eds. de Minuit, 1992), p. 101.

[22] P. Claudel, *Positions and propositions,* vol. 2 (Paris: Gallimard, 1942), p. 174.

The final moment of this path, to date (and into the future, by the grace of God!), *L'arche de la parole* (1998), considers praise, and thus the *thank you* and the *yes,* as the highest possibility of speech, which once again makes the latter responsive and vocative. This book shows that the human body does not respond solely by itself and for itself, that its task and dignity are to speak for all that does not speak, to be the place where the world transforms its light into song. Human dialogue lives only in also being a response to things and to the world. Such are the command and the compassion of the song.

To conclude, two clarifications and a word of thanks. On one hand, the abundance of references to various authors and the frequency of proper names in these works have sometimes occasioned astonishment. But leaving aside the fact that the practice of not recognizing one's sources and debts does not become more elegant when one is lavish about them, one might simply ask whether it is possible to affirm that the human voice is polyphonic, even in its singularity, open in the most intimate way to other voices, unless this affirmation is also put to work? In the same way, it is not possible to affirm that the essence of speech is praise unless the speech that makes that affirmation has itself come to praise. Concerning, on the other hand, the relations of philosophy and theology, simple good sense suffices for one to see that the only act calling for critique would be the one that confuses the two (and in two senses! There are theologians who are in fact only philosophers). There is nothing at all contentious in what the same author writes of philosophy *and* theology, which is the case here. The criterion of theology is to be expressly under the *lumen fidei,* in the light of faith, and thus in obedience to the Word of God—a trying obedience, since it is one that will always fall short of the excess of what it must hear. This criterion suffices to discriminate which among the diverse works evoked here belong to philosophy and which to theology. As for the internal articulation, it resides in the fact that it is possible, as many philosophers have thought, that philosophy poses questions to which it cannot respond in ultimate fashion, and that philosophy cannot close on itself. One is certainly at liberty to say (but one must also demonstrate this) that such questions are badly posed, or that they have no response. It is also possible (and indeed, by saying this one does it) to seek the response in another source, and to examine what light harks back to it.

A *merci,* at last. At the origin of this path, though none of it can be charged to his course of reflection, was—by his presence, his words, his writings, and in short his *existence*—Henri Maldiney, luminous example of rigor and attention. It is from the bottom of my heart that I thank him.

Paris, November 1999

OTHER BOOKS BY JEAN-LOUIS CHRÉTIEN

Lueur du secret (Paris: Eds. de L'Herne, 1985)
L'effoi du beau (Paris: Eds. du Cerf, 1987, second edition 1997)
Traversées de l'imminence (Paris: Eds. de L'Herne, 1989)
L'antiphonaire de la nuit (Paris: Eds. de L'Herne, 1989)
La voix nue. Phénoménologie de la promesse (Paris: Eds. de Minuit, 1990)
Loins des premiers fleuves (Paris: Eds. de la Différence, 1990)
L'appel et la réponse (Paris: Eds. de Minuit, 1992)
Parmi les eaux violentes (Paris: Mercure de France, 1993)
Effractions brèves (Paris: Obsidiane, 1995)
De la fatigue (Paris: Eds. de Minuit, 1996)
Corps à corps. À l'écoute de l'oeuvre de l'art (Paris: Eds. de Minuit, 1997)
Entre flèche et cri (Paris: Obsidiane, 1998)
L'arche de la parole (Paris: P. U. F., 1998, second edition 1999)
Le regard de l'amour (Paris: Desclée de Brouwer, 2000)

INDEX OF NAMES